DATE DUE

JE 7 '05			

DEMCO 38-296

A CLASS OF THEIR OWN
When Children Teach Children

Dennie Briggs

Foreword by Arthur Gillette

BERGIN & GARVEY
Westport, Connecticut • London

Library of Congress Cataloging-in-Publication Data

Briggs, Dennie.
    A class of their own : when children teach children / Dennie
Briggs.
        p. cm.
    Includes bibliographical references (p.) and index.
    ISBN 0–89789–550–9 (hardcover : alk. paper). —ISBN 0–89789–563–0
(pbk. : alk. paper)
    1. Peer-group tutoring of students—United States. l. Title.
LB1031.5.B75 1998
371.39′4—dc21   97–41000

British Library Cataloguing in Publication Data is available.

Library of Congress Catalog Card Number: 97–41000
ISBN: 0–89789–550–9
        0–89789–563–0 (pbk.)

First published in 1998

Bergin & Garvey, 88 Post Road West, Westport, CT 06881
An imprint of Greenwood Publishing Group, Inc.

Printed in the United States of America

The paper used in this book complies with the
Permanent Paper Standard issued by the National
Information Standards Organization (Z39.48–1984).

10 9 8 7 6 5 4 3 2 1

For
Alice Cutting,
Wayne Hunnicutt,
Madison Lowe,
and
Rodney Odgers,
students who became my teachers

Nursery Rhyme

Happy childhood is an adult fable
Recited to those who, as yet unable
To discern what is and what is not,
Readily accept what they are taught.
—John M. Maher

Contents

Foreword: "So Simple Only a Child Can Do It"

Some years ago, I found myself in Gibraltar on a 26–foot sailboat poised for a cruise first to the Canary Islands and from there—deep breath—to the West Indies.

Ámitie, the cutter, was shipshape and sound of hull and rigging, her sails were tough, we had the right charts, the weather and winds promised no scares in the weeks just ahead, and my two shipmates and I were psyched to go.

There was only one hitch—and a major one at that.

In those days before Geographical Positioning System began giving sailors a satellite fix true down to 10 meters anywhere in the world on an instrument the size of a cellular phone, sextant-based navigation was still an absolute must for crossing an ocean, beyond the reach of the shore radio beacons we had hitherto depended on in British, then Mediterranean, waters.

The hitch? *None of us had the faintest idea how to use a sextant.*

Learning how fell to me—and I've sometimes wondered if that straw-draw wasn't rigged by my companions.

Be that as it may, I left them the final pre-Atlantic carpentry and sail stitching and set to poring over nautical almanacs, cruising guides, and other sailing texts. This was a frustrating and increasingly jittery—because totally unsuccessful—attempt to fathom the Fine Art and Exact Science of the Sextant.

"If the Arab sailors could learn how to use one over a millenium ago (I'd seen a fine ninth-century parchment specimen in the museum at Fez, Morocco), why the so-and-so can't I?" I ruminated.

Time was of the essence since (1) the fair-weather tradewind season was beginning to draw to a close, with the danger of dead calms—or hurricanes!—starting to loom on our much-desired western horizon, and (2) we hadn't the resources to wait until the next tradewind season.

"Well," I reasoned, "our ninth-century Arab seamen-forebears were probably illiterate and, in any event, had no nautical almanacs or cruising guides at their disposal. So how did they learn to use a sextant? "

Lightbulb!

And that evening found me comfortably ensconced in the cabin of a neighboring sailboat at the Gib yacht basin, listening to Verdi's *Requiem* with one ear and her captain with the other. I soaked up in a couple of hours more about King Sextant than I had gleaned from several days of frenzied reading.

This particular "class of our own" got *Ámitie* to the Canaries safely, albeit a mite off course—the beauty of Verdi had doubtless distracted my attention just as one or two finer points were being explained. But I had brushed up and practiced as our little ship swung to her anchor in Las Palmas, and then imparted the new skill to my mates in less time than it takes to say "Yo-ho-ho and a bottle of rum!" or "What shall we do with a drunken sailor?"

This bit of roll-over mutual apprenticeship in what was—quite literally—a survival skill saw *Ámitie* 2,700 nautical miles to Barbados with a terminal error of some 5 nautical miles.

Peer teaching? You don't have to convince me!

And I've often wondered why on earth (or at sea) large enterprises, not to mention government administrations (including—ahem—ministries of education), don't have the generalized and systematic practice of cross-referenced computer files of peer teaching supply and demand. I for one would gladly exchange a couple of after-work hours a week transmitting my modicum of Russian language skills to someone who could minister mercifully to my pitiful guitar plunking—I'd even supply the ear plugs!

"OK for self-possessed adults," you may be thinking, "but what about *mere kids!?*"

Experience shows that "mere," in this context, is something of a self-fulfilling prophecy: Condition a youngster to perceive him/herself as irresponsible, incapable, etc., and that's the behavior you'll probably get.

Witness *a contrario* the tens of thousands of teenagers who mobilized, with preservice training and in-service backstopping, to reduce illiteracy during the Cuban (1960) and Nicaraguan (1980) national literacy campaigns. They succeeded because—like the Little Engine chugging up that mountain—they were challenged to think they could.

Witness, as well, my 20-year-old son whose Sorbonne Students' UNESCO Club spent a year providing weekly sessions of remedial support at a multiethnic junior high school in a Paris neighborhood politely described as "difficult." "Hey, Dad," he said to me the other day, "we helped out in geography and history. But those kids have certainly taught us as much as, if not more than, we've taught them."

With ever-faster evolving technologies and pedagogical methods, there may, in fact, be areas where adults are less effective teachers than young-sters. My son has taught his mother more about word processing than the other way around.

And then there was the affirmation by 1950s Harvard-professor-turned-nightclub *chansonnier* Tom Lehrer to the effect that New Math was "so simple *only* a child can do it."

Arthur Gillette*
Director,
Division of Youth and Sports Activities,
UNESCO

*Provided in a personal capacity.

Introduction

Your own teachers are all around you: they're available to you if you know how to approach them. And the wisdom that you will gain will make you sound like one of the great prophets of all time.

Michael Harner

The current push to increase literacy in schools offers an unprecedented opportunity to address a number of pressing social issues simultaneously. In addition to reducing illiteracy, we could revitalize public education as we know it and bring about significant changes in the way children and young people learn. We could change the way teachers instruct. Furthermore, we could modify how older and younger children view each other. And finally, we could bridge the gap between generations leading to a more vital, human existence for us all.

President Clinton, in various campaign appearances, outlined a number of initiatives that included a three-pronged approach to learning: improve literacy at an early age, provide entry to technology for all young people, and, finance universal higher education. He further urged wide-scale community service for high school students.

To carry out this ambitious undertaking, he suggested the mobilization of an "army of tutors" (work-study high school and college students, AmeriCorps personnel, parents, and reading specialists).

But nowhere did the president mention what children themselves could contribute to teaching others, to make their schooling more vital, or to contribute to the improvement of society. We still see children as mere passive beneficiaries of older people's efforts. And yet there is remarkable evidence of what they can do.

Teachers know the powerful effects of teaching. Sociologists more than half a century ago discovered that principle. As they worked with delinquents, they found that prisoners could help one another (similar to Alcoholics Anonymous); more important, the counseling prisoner was more apt to change his own criminality than the one he was helping. Researchers of the treatment of addicts came to the same conclusion. The idea was not to diminish the prisoner's or addict's power but to find legitimate ways that she or he could use it.

The same applies to children and young people. They have experienced schooling and know what has been useful and who have been effective teachers. They know many shortcuts to learning.

In this book, I will address the issue of children making a significant contribution to teaching other children in collaboration with young people, teachers, and other adults. This method of peer teaching will focus on how to train children to tutor, how to use different methods of instruction, and how to evaluate learning. This focus will feature teaching basic communication skills. Examples from numerous settings will illustrate the fundamental method, then I will pose other areas where peer teachers can use their talents. Finally, I will suggest how peer teaching can become an integral part of mainstream learning and what impact it could have.

The problem with educational reform is that essentially it's been an "add-on," more-of-the-same, strategy rather than one of basic change. Politicians and administrators add on "new" courses for both teachers and pupils. Educational administrators add on "new" teaching devices, "new" classrooms, "new" dress codes, and "new" disciplinary measures. But teacher-led instruction in self-contained classrooms remains the basic format.

The president's initiatives, as commendable as they are, remain as yet more add-on tactics. According to Herbert Kohl he is "recognizing the right problem while proposing the wrong solution. . . . There is some disconnection between children and texts that takes place at school, and there is no reason to believe that sending volunteers into the early grades on an episodic basis will be more useful than any of the other efforts made at increasing literacy among the poor."[1]

The initiatives, however, could go much further. Getting more young people into the classroom itself could have an enormous effect on improving learning. But their presence could also threaten teachers. For years I've heard teachers lament about the size of their classrooms and how they wished they could individualize instruction. The recent California mandate for smaller class sizes beginning immediately in kindergarten through grade three, offers teachers an incredible opportunity to change the way they teach. What I fear is another "add-on," quick-fix to the problem: They will continue their traditional methodology merely with fewer students in additional portable classrooms.

We hear figures reflecting that 40 percent of third graders are not able to read on their own or that three-quarters of fourth graders are not able to read at their grade level. There are projections that 7 million more children will enter schools in the next decade while the number of fourteen to seventeen year olds will increase by 20 percent. And all that growth will require an estimated 3 million new teachers.

What I'm advocating is a change of structure in the classroom—it isn't simply adding another "intervention," aide, or gadget for the teacher, but involves a change in the relationship between teachers and students and our expectations of their behavior. "Even more intriguing than improvement in learning are the changes in social behavior, motivation, attitudes, and self-concept occurring in the child doing the tutoring. The tutor frequently shows a better attitude toward school and teachers, becomes more responsible, and thinks more highly of himself."[2]

What we need is a "loaves and fishes" plan—a way to transform what we already have into something far greater. Instead of merely putting 100,000 work-study students into the classrooms to teach reading, I propose a three-tiered plan. It would begin with:

1. *Preparing Trainers*. Education professors would teach AmeriCorps, Teacher Corps, and work-study college students how to teach. Students have had many teachers through the years, so they already know a lot about effective learning conditions.

The trainers would also learn how to monitor tutoring programs, carry out quality control functions, conduct advanced training, and fashion ways to evaluate progress with each student—and each tutor as well. They would be trained in ancillary functions such as fund-raising, augmenting public relations, and forming networks.

2. *Developing Master Tutors*. These trainers would then serve as core staff who would teach community college and high school students how to teach younger students (who would do the actual tutoring). These trainers, supported by their professors, would visit the tutorial sites to offer on-the-job assistance and continual training.

3. *Building a Vast Reservoir of Tutors*. These master tutors, in turn, would teach older children (middle school, fourth through sixth graders) to tutor in Head Start, and kindergarten through third grade and be their coaches.

The classroom teachers would collaborate with the tutors and master tutors to design and implement individualized programs. The children and young people would bring fresh ideas along with teaching skills into the classroom; they would contribute drive and enthusiasm for doing new things.

Classroom teachers would benefit manifoldly. For one thing, relieved of instructing many of the basics, they could devote more time individually to children who needed it. They could learn more about new teaching methods (such as creative use of computers, video, and other forms of technology). Teachers would need to learn management and training skills and do more of their work as a team. But, in turn, they would witness the accomplishment of seeing more educational objectives realized than previously.

President Clinton's literacy initiative, America Reads, is one of a series of child-focused proposals: "The most important thing we have to do is make sure our children are ready for the 21st century," the *New York Times* reported on August 28, 1996. The president continued, "All America's children should be able to read on their own by the third grade." America Reads calls for $1.45 billion for the employment of reading specialists, $2.5 billion for after-school and summer tutoring, $1 billion for AmeriCorps personnel, and another $300 million to train parents to help their children. By redeploying these funds, the participants, including tutors of younger children, could receive payment for their work. Rates would be determined by the level of skill that they reached. And so the plan would embody crucial employment objectives as well as those of teaching and learning.

PROVISO

I have reviewed literally hundreds of pieces about peer teaching that ranged from descriptive accounts to research documents. Teachers have frequently adopted peer teaching as another device to manipulate children into doing their own work. Many of the programs (and some are widespread) are based on behavioral conditioning; reinforced with points, rewards and punishments; measured in terms of standardized tests; and so on. These tactics foster still more competition between children. And so I've chosen not to focus on these approaches. They are well documented in the literature; any teacher will find them easy to use and complete with manuals, videotapes, exercises, tests, certificates, etc. Harvard's Jerome Bruner wrote, "External reinforcement may indeed get a particular act going and may even lead to its repetition, but it does not nourish, reliably, the long course of learning."[3] My intention here is to concentrate on the more human side of peer teaching. Instruction, as Bruner says, is fundamentally a social process, a matter of relationships—to people, things, and ideas.[4]

Whether one is a devotee of classical education or a less-structured one where children are free to use imaginations, peer teaching can enhance either approach. The content is not as consequential as the relationship between the tutor and student and the degree of freedom they have to explore learning.

I chose my life, or rather, it chose me, to be involved in action-followed-by-reflection. My goal in writing this book is to stir the imagination and encourage people to design a democratic curriculum by participation. I've tried to let peer teachers, teachers, and students speak for themselves as much as possible through vignettes of their conversations, discussions, and critiques of their work. I wrote this book not primarily as an academic one, yet I bestow it with scholarship. I intend it as a beginning source—a draft copy—for teachers, parents, and students to get them started. Hopefully, it will attract some conscientious young people who want to serve by teaching and helping others.

As the president listened to two children read to him at a campaign stop, little did he realize that these same children could be our most effective tutors to assist the 3 million new teachers we will soon need. And we could address a host of other social issues as well.

I would like to thank my brother, Bob, for his contribution to preparing this book. While we do not see eye-to-eye on all its conclusions, he nonetheless has helped me to consider other perspectives and shaped its form.

I am grateful to Jane Garry, acquisitions editor; Arlene Belzer, production editor; and Sally Hemingway, copyeditor; for all their assistance.

A CLASS OF
THEIR OWN

1

A Very Natural Thing

Reading is to the mind what exercise is to the body.
Richard Steele (1672–1729), *The Tattler*

Contrary to popular belief, most of the world's children learn the basic skills of communication and survival from one another. Older children pass on the shortcuts they've learned by trial-and-error to their juniors along with those aspects of their culture that they have found useful to become more independent: elementary things like how to put on your clothes, what to avoid, how to manipulate adults. Most of this on-the-job learning occurs in the family and the neighborhood. It's not all positive though, for children also learn to exploit younger ones and enjoy the power they can exert over them.

Formal education has a long tradition of children teaching younger ones. The teacher in the one-room school, which characterized our early educational system, relied on this technique. As far back as fourteenth-century Europe, a renowned school master made his best "elder scholars" teachers of the younger ones. And by the seventeenth century, England had thousands of pupil teachers, many of them paid. The most extensive venture in modern times, however, occurred in the 1960s as part of Cuba's "Year of Education." President Castro closed the nation's schools for six months while volunteer pupil-teachers all but eradicated illiteracy among adults in that short time.

During the 1960s and 1970s, some educators revived the practice in this country. Teacher shortages and the impetus for increasing literacy in programs such as Head Start led to wide-scale programs that employed peer or cross-age teaching. It was during this era that I first became involved in peer teaching.

When I was substitute teaching in a combined second and third grade class, the children became highly motivated to read after some sixth grade "problem" children came to help out in our room. They saw older children, whom they had formerly feared, share reading skills with them and, in so doing, learned to be more patient themselves. The partnership included thinking up ways to make learning exciting and, as a result, fun.

It all began at nine o'clock one morning when the door opened and twelve-year-old Bill stood defiantly on the threshold of our portable classroom. All thirty-two children turned to see who it was. After a sudden silence, a controlled panic spread through the room. Then all the children busied themselves intensively.

"Oh, Mr. B," Alan finally said, "There's someone at the door to see *you!*"

The principal of the school in southern California wondered if some of the older boys sent to her for disciplinary action might be able to help out in the classrooms.

"Often they're just bored and so they torment the younger children," she told me. We discussed the idea, and I agreed to take one boy as an experiment. But I didn't know that the principal would act this soon, or that it would be Bill.

I had no idea of how to work with Bill. Often I had seen him sitting outside the principal's office. He was tall, with curly brown hair and large blue eyes that looked at you with a directness disconcerting in a sixth grader. He was a known bully among the 800 children at the school.

Caught off guard, I merely introduced him as if his reputation didn't exist and said that he was going to help out in our room. I'd actually violated one of my own principles—that of discussing any proposed changes—so that the children could be involved. I had planned to discuss this possibility, but before I could, the principal had acted. I invited him to sit next to me in the circle as we commenced our usual morning planning session.

Bill stayed all day. Intuitively, he seemed to understand what we were doing and pitched in to help the children with their studies. He stayed after class, and we went over some of the things he might do. I don't recall the details, but I do remember that I asked him if he had younger brothers or sisters. He was the youngest. Then, could he think back to what it was like when he was eight or nine, what was difficult for him in school, and what was fun?

He came back the next day and the next. By the end of the week, the two smallest boys in our class asked if he could be their regular teacher.

Reading and grammar had been difficult for Bill—ironically, the two areas these boys wanted help with. So Bill had to enlist the aid of his older sister.

Bill remained after school each afternoon to have a "teacher's meeting" with me. He wanted to know how he was doing and any tips I could give him. And mornings he would wait for me outside the portable to go over last minute plans. One morning he appeared with a wooden case—his "learning kit"—which he'd made to carry his teaching materials.

All went well until his first crisis. Bill announced to his two students that he was taking them on a "learning walk." Equipped with his kit and a boy on each hand, they were off to look for nouns.

Half an hour later they returned, one of the boys crying, Bill tense and shaking. The boy had run off to play while Bill insisted they proceed with their lesson. When apprehended, Bill had given him a good cuffing.

A rough enough youngster himself, just approaching adolescence, Bill became frightened when he saw the smaller boy's reaction to his attempts at discipline. Discouraged, Bill was on the verge of giving up teaching.

We role-played what had happened. The other children gave their views and suggested different ways Bill could have handled the situation. And then we role-played these fresh solutions while Bill and his students watched, now and then adding their ideas.

Other "problem boys" came to help our class. Finally we got some girls. The children readily accepted the new teachers. Eventually we had a one-to-three ratio. Our noon brown-bag "teacher's seminar" now numbered twelve, most of them boys.

The new teachers looked for guidance to Bill, who'd become their consultant. At first they chose "hard core" subjects that they themselves had only recently mastered—reading, spelling, writing, and math. Later, they ventured into other areas such as physical education, social studies, music, and art. The whole class looked forward to Bill's science demonstrations.

I found a high school student who wanted to help; he and Bill established an individualized "professional" athletics program for the children and brought in other high school students.

Family ties also changed as parents saw their children become more interested in learning. Bill's mother telephoned me one day to say he demanded the television be shut off during certain hours as it was interfering with his lesson planning. Previously he had been a television addict. Now he was getting along better with his older sister whose help he needed on occasion.

What I didn't expect was that the seven and eight year olds in time would want to follow in the footsteps of their tutors. When the children became more accustomed to having the older children as tutors, some wanted to help out in the kindergarten. They spent an hour each day practicing their new skills by reading to the children in small groups and playing with them on their playground. And they met with the kindergarten teacher for their own brown-bag seminar, which included Bill as their consultant.

My pleasure at the eagerness and struggles they showed to tailor their newfound reading abilities to younger ones was nearly quashed by Shirley, a somewhat overgrown girl for her age and viewed at the school as "strange." She showed up at our "teachers' meeting" one day after the kindergarten teacher asked for more tutors. The tutors, to my amazement, accepted her pledge on face value, and began to incorporate her into their tutorial. They pointed out that the book she had chosen was far too advanced for five year olds. Oddly enough, when she began teaching, the youngsters listened to her and, in time, she chose stories that they could grasp.

What was more amazing was that her school attendance increased remarkably. Previously, she was often absent; now she had daily responsibility for her group—and to attend the teachers' meetings. She had ups and downs, of course, but overall, her behavior changed so remarkably, her mother came to see the principal. The mother had told the principal that I was no longer giving Shirley her daily medications (a psychiatrist had diagnosed Shirley as autistic and she was in our room while waiting placement in a mental institution). In reality, we found she was an exceptional child and, at the end of the year, the principal agreed that we advance her a grade.

How did the parents react to cross-age teaching? In order to familiarize parents with what we were doing, I invited them to come to a meeting one evening. I borrowed video equipment and taped some sessions with the children to show them, thinking that, informally over coffee, we could discuss the project and see what they thought about it. But to my surprise, over 100 parents, friends, and children showed up—more than had ever attended PTA meetings at that school; we had no room to accommodate them all, so had to hold our session on the lawn outside. Only one mother objected to having her child being tutored by another, and so I arranged to have her child transferred to a different classroom. Another mother came to see me at year's end. The family was moving to another area, and she asked if I would write a letter of recommendation for her daughter so that she could continue to teach at her next school.

As for Bill, he never returned to his own classroom (much to the relief of his teacher). It was near the end of the school year. He'd become a mentor and role model for the others. He visited classrooms in neighboring schools to pick up new ideas to share in our teachers' seminar. Given freedom, he'd acquired an enormous amount of responsibility by having it. And somehow he kept abreast of his own studies, took his finals, and passed with high grades.

Peer teaching, of course, isn't new. Around 1531, Valentine Trotzendorf (a school dropout due to poverty) is known to have initiated the idea of having children teaching each other. He studied under Luther and eventually became rector of the Goldberg School in Silesia. The best way to learn, he claimed, was to teach and so made his best "elder scholars" teachers of the younger ones. Each day the pupils reviewed what they had learned the previous day. Pupils composed two exercises each week: one in poetry, the other in prose. He carried out peer teaching, however, within a particular context; he democratized his school by establishing a "consul" of twelve "senators," chosen by the boys, who assisted him in handling discipline. The reputation of the Goldberg School spread over Germany and reportedly a large number of the leaders of the next generation were taught there.

In 1798, in the United Kingdom, a Quaker school master opened a school for children of the poor. Unable to hire teachers, he was obliged to recruit his staff from among the pupils and developed a monitorial-tutorial system. From 1848 onwards, pupil-teachers were officially recognized throughout that country and by 1870, more than 34,000 were known to be involved, many of them being paid for their services. The practice was an important one for recruiting and training teachers.

Similar developments occurred in this country during the 1860s. One educator commented, "By teaching the younger children, the more advanced are constantly reviewing their studies, not by learning merely, but by the surer method of teaching what they have learned to others."[1]

Fast forward 100 years.

During the 1960s, many projects (the federal government's funding encouraged some projects aimed at reducing the gap between the poor and the middle classes) made extensive use of peer teaching. Two University of Michigan professors, Peggy and Ronald Lippitt, carried out one of the most extensive projects. They carefully instituted and studied the teaching and resulting socialization processes in operation in several school systems. In their studies, older children taught youngers—cross-age teaching. The Lippitts prepared extensive teacher-training and evaluation methods from the studies.[2]

Another program, the Mobilization for Youth after-school tutoring project in New York City's schools, paid 1,500 tutors for their work with 4,500 children.[3] The National Commission on the Resources for Youth conducted a third large-scale project (Youth Tutoring Youth) operating after school hours and in the summer collaborating with the Neighborhood Youth Corps. In this program, children, two years behind their grade level in reading, became tutors to younger children, who were also below achievement. The Ford Foundation funded a large-scale project (The Tutorial Community) in a Los Angeles area with a high population of Latino children. One elementary school incorporated peer teaching in all its classrooms, not as a remedial procedure, but as part of its regular teaching methods. Children helped one another in the same classrooms: older children taught those younger, junior high school students tutored the children in the upper grades, and tutors went to other schools to help out. Parents reinforced the efforts at home.[4] There were many other projects.

But it was Cuba that carried out the most extensive program in 1961, during President Fidel Castro's "Year of Education." The goal was to eliminate illiteracy among adults, a goal that remarkably 271,000 volunteer youth tutoring 700,000 adults nearly accomplished in only six months. Illiteracy was reduced from 23.6 percent to 3.9 percent.

> Equipped with hammocks, lanterns and specially produced adult primers, the *brigadistas* fanned out into the countryside, where most Cubans lived then—and where the illiteracy was twice the national average.
>
> Wherever they went, they set to work at once motivating the people to learn, teaching them, testing their progress and tabulating the results for inclusion in national statistics.[5]
>
> [One] decade later, a healthy percentage of the country's educational personnel is made up of brigade veterans. There are numerous teachers and even headmasters of 25 or 26 for whom participation in the campaign was a vocational and personal turning point. Through it, they learned a kind of literacy in social awareness.[6]

Since then, the practice has become mainstream in the schools. Classes elect those students who are best at each subject and have demonstrated the skill to teach.[7]

Peer teaching is fundamental in international programs such as the Peace Corps, the United Kingdom's Community Services Volunteers, International Volunteers Services, and by *Freres des Hommes* in Europe.

I had the good fortune to visit a unique school, the *Freinet école*, where peer teaching was not only incorporated into the mainstream, but was the norm. Sitting on a hillside in the St. Paul de Vence region of southern France are a cluster of whitewashed, clapboard, one-story buildings amidst a grove of eucalyptus and mimosa trees. Two nondescript dogs wandered about. Through one door of a building I could hear children singing. When my ear had focused more clearly, other sounds were emitted— strange, improvised tones. I thought I heard a swarm of bees and then there was a loud crescendo, which I learned later was a spider. I peeked inside the open door to see two eleven- and twelve-year-old boys rehearsing an opera they had written. Some older children had helped them modify instruments including an old piano to get the special sound effects they desired.

In another room, children were making large puppets with heads of *papier mâché*. In yet another building, a dozen or so children were seated in a circle where an older boy gave them a "conference" on the results of his studies into how automobiles work. Children were attentive and critical of his presentation, including the posters he'd made to illustrate his talk. A boy said one of the charts was not accurate and showed him where he'd made a mistake. In the next building, two boys were seated in a corner, one teaching mathematics to the other while two adolescent girls read in another part of the room. A good-looking young man in his early twenties wearing shorts and sandals sat cross-legged in the middle of the floor studying. I found out he was a nominal "teacher" who'd come from Paris for the year to live in and work at this boarding school. His role, as I was to learn, more resembled that of a foreman than the traditional one of a teacher.

I was introduced to M. Bertaloo, the headmaster, who told me about his school which had five to sixteen year olds. The children worked on their own projects. They planned what they were going to do, how to go about it, and listed what help in the form of materials and instruction they would need. They presented a time frame that included a tentative date for their "conference." The children themselves did most of the teaching. It seemed like the natural thing to do. Each child, therefore, had to figure out who had the knowledge or skills they needed for their project and then negotiate for their services. They could also go outside the school to seek assistance from people in the community.

There was an interesting structure that had evolved over the years since Célestin Freinet established this school in 1927 (operated privately until 1991, when it became part of the French educational system as an "experimental school"). He originally saw it as a kind of "trial-and-error" learning. For discussion and making decisions, he organized the school into groups of about twenty-five children—a kind of "class cooperative." All the staff and students held a weekly assembly where they could hold debates for matters that affected the school and its operations.[8]

In the mid-1960s, a number of my extension students at the University of California, Riverside, wanted to have the opportunity to try peer teaching on a schoolwide basis. We obtained a grant from the U.S. Office of Economic Opportunity to operate a summer school for about 200 children for this purpose. We found a rural ghetto area in which the idea was acceptable. Most of the children came from homes whose only income was welfare, and their test scores in reading, math and so on, were about two years behind the norms. We had eight teachers and thirty-two peer teachers (paraprofessionals—youth and a few adults) who were paid. The paraprofessional group was composed of eight each: high school and college students, school dropouts, and parents. The children, who volunteered for the summer school, ranged in age from four to twelve. Instead of traditional grouping by age (with the exception of the preschoolers), the children selected a "cluster" they wanted to be with for the six weeks. Clusters consisted of about twenty-five children of all ages, a teacher and four assistants. In a sense, each cluster became a small learning community; each took on its own individual characteristics.

A unique feature was a "change and development team," composed of two New Careerists (former felons, recently paroled from the California Department of Corrections), a graduate student, and myself as its coordinator. The team was involved in training the staff, monitoring the project, and evaluating it. The project director likened the team's functions to a thermostat that:

> collects data about how hot or cold it is and decides when to turn the air conditioner on or when to turn the furnace on. . . feeding its [observations] back at appropriate times in the program (3:00 seminar) perhaps, and also in the teaching teams. . . . There is something that comes from being outside the group that helps one see what's going on inside it and it helps him know what he might do better at a future time.[9]

Peer teaching occurred within and among clusters. Subjects ranged from basic communication skills to science, arts, recreation, sports, and field trips. I'll have more to say about this project in later chapters.

With the growth of the teacher-training industry, the formalization of professional standards, unionization, and the struggle for recognition and power among teachers, the model of the lone teacher in a self-contained classroom became the dominating one and still remains. As recently as 1974, a study of 110 one-teacher schools in the state of Nebraska found that nearly one-third of the students said they had some form of regular peer tutoring while for another one-fourth it was informal. More than three-fourths of the students replied that they asked other students for help and 88 percent said they worked together with another student on their schoolwork.[10] In the developing countries where there is less separation between living and educating, peer teaching is the most common form of learning. There is the danger that this method, which is so basic, will become extinct in the ensuing struggle as educators take on the formalized nature which dominates most of the industrialized countries.

Peer teaching provides individualized instruction as well as increases the motivation to learn. The participants can recognize different learning and teaching styles and put them into practice. Children who learn more slowly have a chance to advance without feeling left out. Children who learn faster can put their skills to work tutoring younger ones. Children see their peer teacher as a friend—a "buddy" whom they can look up to. Teachers are able to spend more time with children who need it the most.

Older children talk the language of the younger child. They know what was difficult for them at that age and what brought joy. At the same time, the practice allows for peer teachers to change their image to that of a partner and attainable role model. Attitudes of trust, love, and caring emerge. They learn positive leadership skills. As many soon find out, the teaching experience fosters creativity and exposes tutors to deficits in their own learning. One group of fourth graders in Texas, for example, not having suitable textbooks, wrote their own (which included poems, limericks, and riddles) for their first graders—books they could check out and take home for further study. And in so doing, the peer teachers found many words and concepts they didn't know. It's not only children who can benefit. College athletes at the University of Texas, who lacked academic requirements and were being tutored by fellow students, were paired with underachieving students at an elementary school. By the end of the year, both the athletes and the children not only improved their academic records, but also developed a heightened interest in self-motivated learning.

As for teachers, when peer tutors begin to empathize with the dilemmas of their own teachers, the relationship changes to that of colleagues engaged in exciting new learning adventures. Both teacher and peer teacher experience the benefits of cross-generational teamwork in collaborative projects.

In a nutshell, extensive development and use of peer teaching could significantly improve learning for everyone and change the essentially elitist way formal education is offered.

WHAT PEER TEACHING CAN DO FOR YOU

1. Advantages to older children. They learn:

    how to teach specific skills to younger children; how to be helpful; how to put their knowledge to use;

    how to apply their learning and use their own creativity to concoct activities to teach youngers;

    how to relate constructively to younger children; what younger children are like; to be responsible; to contribute as a team in helping others; what it is like to feel needed, useful, and appreciated; valuable work experience;

    parenting and human relations skills; to empathize;

    how to become positive role models; to increase self-esteem, responsibility, trust, love, caring, and compassion; leadership skills; to experience cooperative procedures rather than competitive ones;

    how to gain experience, an apprenticeship (a "head-start") for a career in the helping professions.

2. Advantages to younger children. They learn:

    to work at their own pace on needed subject areas and in the manner that is most useful to them; new things; to see learning in a more positive manner;

    to experience success;

    to change their image of older children positively; to have an older friend;

    and, to students who learn more slowly, to advance and feel successful.

3. Advantages to teachers. They can:

    spend more time with the children who really need it the most;

    give opportunities for more individualized instruction to maximize learning styles and to increase self-motivation to learn;

    obtain an unlimited source of skilled volunteer help; meet the challenges of children who learn faster;

    reduce the generational and professional communication gap between teacher and student; utilize older children who talk the language of their students and thus provide a linkage between children and teachers;

develop mutual appreciation: teachers become colleagues with their peer teachers (peer tutors empathize with the predicaments their own teachers face);

increase the joy in achievement;

set an example of seriousness, importance of learning and teaching (learning is exciting and within reach);

experience the benefits of teamwork;

gain opportunities to evaluate teaching methods and resources.

4. Advantages to parents. They can:
more actively participate in their children's learning through supporting and engaging in their projects;

get more direct access to the classroom, the teachers, and the peer tutors;

open channels of communication across generations, genders, and ethnic groups.

HOW TO USE THIS BOOK

Chapter 2 is concerned with different learning styles and the different forms of intelligence. For those who want to undertake a peer teaching program or see their children in one, chapter 3 is about beginnings: selection of peer teachers and tutors, conducting planning meetings, assessing learning and teaching styles, the teacher's role, when and where to conduct peer teaching. Chapter 4 covers the teaching sessions and reviews. And chapter 5 addresses ways to evaluate and modify a program. These last three chapters will help to get a program going. Finally, chapter 6 gives some possibilities of carrying the peer teacher to higher levels and looks to the future of the self-determined student.

2
One Size Doesn't Fit All

Travelers on the road to ancient Athens were tied to an iron bed by Procrustes, the legendary highwayman of Attica. He would stretch them if they didn't fit, or cut off whatever parts overlapped.

Like the proverbial old woman who lived in a shoe, teachers all across the nation say they have too many children in their classrooms. They want to individualize instruction to meet particular ways of learning for each student. We realize that just as there are multiple intelligences, there are also different ways to learn and to think. At any given age, some children learn best through action. Curiosity, vividness, and restlessness often dominate their waking moments until they gain mastery of their attentions. Some never do. They often learn best through interpersonal experiences. Others have more repose and learn best by didactic instruction and from working on their own. Still others can combine action with reflection.

Likewise, there are a variety of teaching styles. As we all know, finding a good "fit" between teacher and student can spark learning. Children also need variety; so do teachers. Learning is, after all, fundamentally a relationship between people and between people and things that includes ideas.

Everyone can remember their favorite teachers along with those whom they least admired. I got off to a good start in kindergarten by having one of those kind-hearted, motherly types who seemed able to tolerate all our demands without becoming restrictive. My first-grade teacher was orderly and disciplined. I was excited about learning to read. Each day, she got us in small groups of five or six for a reading session; for homework, we had to review what we'd read. She put a rubber band on the remainder of the book, and we weren't allowed to look further. My second-grade teacher, who was rather nondescript, faithfully followed her lesson plans and rarely departed; I don't recall her ever smiling or laughing. I don't even remember her name. But my third- and fourth-grade teachers terrorized us. They were strict disciplinarians who didn't hesitate to smack us with a ruler or isolate us from the others as punishment. When I got to the fifth grade, our teacher was also the principal, and likewise strict—she maintained that she never made a mistake and constantly challenged us to catch her up. She had favorite students and used them to control the rest of us. But I had to wait until the sixth grade to find a teacher who was creative—and a risk-taker. That classroom became a constantly changing and challenging event for her and for us; she was less concerned with lessons and more with application. And we had lots of fun. This teacher would have embraced peer teaching with the same excitement, and my first-grade teacher could certainly have used the help of sixth graders. I would have jumped at the chance to have been a tutor. But I had to wait.

The public's wide acceptance of "therapy," and all the various self-help means, acknowledges our growing need to improve ourselves so we can lead more satisfying lives. The appeal of television talk shows perhaps says that beyond the curiosity and voyeurism, many people are dissatisfied in their relationships with others and want to improve them. Those routes to self-understanding don't work for everyone; in fact, some people become "addicted" to procedures and thus not liberated.

These trends indicate that teachers need to take an active part in developing children's self-awareness and social development so they won't occur on such a haphazard basis. Children have a craving for social learning which we should include legitimately as part of the curriculum, not something either to avoid or tack on. In the long run, educators constantly have to deal with aberrant behavior. Their way usually amounts to a variety of restrictive measures. More recently, we've seen an array of "prevention" strategies. As helpful as they may appear on the surface, prevention still deals with deterring negative social behavior such as substance abuse, delinquency, or teen age pregnancies.

Now what we need is a more positive approach—one that we can integrate with education. Psychologists and educators have long been aware of personal factors which facilitate, or conversely, impede learning. Children need to learn how to comprehend other viewpoints, to be able to shift from one perspective to another as necessary, to tolerate ambiguity, and to be comfortable dealing in abstractions. Fortunately, there are a number of ideas that we can coalesce into new ways of learning. There are recognizable patterns, orientations, or styles of learning, for example, which show themselves early in a child's life that can become assets rather than liabilities. Children form personality configurations, which for most, without regard, remain relatively fixed throughout their lives. And now we are more aware that the ways one learns are not synonymous with intelligence.

The appeal of Daniel Goleman's bestseller, *Emotional Intelligence*, reflects how many people are not content with a narrow definition of intelligence, the kind represented by IQ and scholastic aptitude tests. In an interview, he said, "Emotional intelligence is a different way of being smart. It includes knowing what your feelings are and using your feelings to make good decisions in life. . . . It's empathy; knowing what the people around you are feeling. And it's social skill—getting along well with other people, managing emotions in relationships, being able to persuade or lead others."[1]

He speaks about attaining "emotional" literacy and cites numerous programs around the country that address the need. He wrote, "The common thread is the goal of raising the level of social and emotional competence in children as part of their regular education—not just something taught remedially to children who are faltering and identified as 'troubled,' but a set of skills and understandings essential for every child."[2]

MULTIPLE INTELLIGENCES

More than a decade earlier, Dr. Howard Gardner expanded our limited notion of intelligence in his widely read book, *Frames of Mind: The Theory of Multiple Intelligences*. From his research, he enlarged our understanding by focusing on three main areas of intelligence: (1) that which is related to things which one can see or touch—spacial, logical-mathematical, and bodily—for the main part, measurable,[3] (2) that which is less tangible such as language and music, and (3) that which is personal: intrapersonal and interpersonal.

The personal area is the one which we have neglected in education but have seen in its negative consequences—deviance and disobedience, for instance. Nevertheless we are all aware of the part that emotions play within ourselves and in our relationships with others:

> To feel a certain way—paranoid, envious, jubilant—is to construe a situation in a certain way, to see something as having a possible effect upon oneself or upon other individuals. One may

develop appropriate appraisals, finely honed discriminations, accurate categorizations and classifications of situations; or, less happily, one can make excessively gross discriminations, inappropriate labelings, incorrect inferences, and thus fundamentally misinterpret situations. The less a person understands his own feelings, the more he will fall prey to them. The less a person understands the feelings, the responses, and the behavior of others, the more likely he will interact inappropriately with them and therefore fail to secure his proper place within the larger community.[4]

Furthermore, Gardner maintains that "the personal intelligences are as basic and biological as any intelligences . . . their origins can be discerned in the directly experienced feelings of the individual, in the case of the intrapersonal form, and in the direct perception of significant other individuals, in the case of the interpersonal variety."[5]

Children are curious about the workings of the psyche and need to have accurate information. They are constantly exposed to a wide variety of emotional behavior in their daily lives and from the media. Charles Lee, a sixth grader in Milpitas, California, wrote, "Even in these paranoid times when every person that walks by is considered a potential murderer, there are friends." He wonders if attitude toward other races "was caused by some subconscious prejudice of mine. . . . I, and presumably most people, have a subconscious inclination toward our own people. I just don't have much friendly contact with non-Asians. . . . Our subconscious minds will hinder our efforts to demolish racial borders."[6]

It is in this third area of developing personal intelligence that peer teaching can contribute while simultaneously providing a service. Traditional teaching methods, such as those used to acquire mathematical or language skills, do not "instruct" personal intelligence. Furthermore, personal intelligence is not easily measured. But rather, we can address it in different ways which puts tutelage into a larger framework. "Authorities generally agree," Gardner reminds us, "that, outside of schooled settings, children acquire skills through observation and participation in the contexts in which these skills are customarily invoked."[7] In the standard classroom, Gardner summarizes:

> [T]eachers talk, often presenting material in abstract symbolic form and relying on inanimate media such as books and diagrams in order to convey information. Schooling generally

treats subject matter that one cannot readily see or touch, even as those sensory modes of taking in information seem singularly inappropriate for most school tasks (except for the visual act of reading). Children skilled in the ways of school are accustomed to the presentation of problems and tasks, often out of context, and learn to tackle these assignments just because they are there.[8]

Personal intelligence (which encompasses the wider concept of social intelligence) is a complex element embedded in our daily lives that enhances growth in other areas. "[I]t makes more sense to think of knowledge of self and others as being a higher level, a more integrated form of intelligence, one more at the behest of the culture and of historical factors, one more truly emergent, one that ultimately comes to control and to regulate more 'primary orders' of intelligence."[9]

What peer teaching involves is the construction of simple (but not simplistic) interpersonal contexts in which we can recognize and cultivate personal intelligence.

SOCIAL LEARNING

Moving to the interpersonal area, British psychiatrist Maxwell Jones evolved the concept of "social learning" from his work in therapeutic communities. In these "communities" he created endless opportunities for maximizing relationships within an open, free-flowing structure.

> The term social learning describes the little understood process of change which may result from interpersonal interaction, when some conflict or crisis is analyzed in a group situation, using whatever psychodynamic skills are available. . . . The concept of social learning implies social interaction around some problem area. . . . To achieve such a group climate requires a social structure where the sanctions are positive and there is no threat from the abuse of authority. . . . The concept of social learning implies that the teacher is himself an integral part of the learning process.[10]

Dr. Jones called learning by participation and through action "living-learning" situations. "Teaching and social learning," he wrote, "are both essential ingredients of any educational system." People are cast into real activities, learn on-the-job, and through these interactions—in group discussion and analysis—social learning occurs. He believed that structural aspects (an open, democratic organization) are more important than the skills even highly trained professionals bring to the task. "Cross-age teaching makes use of this potential to train older children to act as socializing agents in their relationships with younger ones. . . . Cross-age teaching points to a possible way of making far greater use of the potential for learning when children are trained to observe and modify their attitudes toward other children.[11]

When I spoke with Dr. Jones, he said:

> The process of social learning is partly one of incorporation. In a setting where older children are teaching younger ones this can happen—the younger ones look up to the older ones who are their teachers, incorporating those traits they admire. Then if the younger ones also have the opportunity to teach other children who are younger than themselves, they can put these new characteristics into practice. And so you see that the relationships among these children can become quite different from the competitive and exploitative ones found so often in the typical school or family.[12]

PERSONALITY TYPES

Personality types have long concerned both psychologists and teachers, the latter in terms of creating optimum learning conditions. One such concept is that of "integration levels" (I-levels), developed by a group of psychologists who were working with navy and marine corps offenders and their treatment. They devised a seven-point scale on which to rate people according to successive levels of interpersonal relationships under which they operated, a kind of "core personality."[13]

> Over a period of time a relatively consistent set of expectations and attitudes is established as a kind of interpreting and working philosophy of life. It is this nexus of gradually expanding experience, expectations, hypotheses, and perceptions which makes up the core of personality. Communication and social interaction are crucial determinants in the development of this core, helping to expand and elaborate the basic potential with which a person is born.[14]

According to their concept, interaction begins with simple, egocentric, self-directed responses and is expanded with experience as the child interacts socially. When a child moves up on their scale, she or he is increasingly able to differentiate between the self and others, increase involvement with others, make discriminations, tolerate ambiguities, and integrate new experiences. "As these discriminations are made and assimilated, a cognitive restructuring of experience and expectancy takes place. A new reference scheme is then developed; a new level of integration is achieved."[15] At each level, there is a better approximation of "reality" than in the previous one—more degrees of freedom and a better understanding of the world around oneself. A greater awareness, empathetic understanding (as differentiated from sympathy), intuitive powers, and an expanded perception of roles follows.

Children, however, can become arrested at any level which then dominates their lives; this fixation is born out in how they see their relationships with others and in the choices they make to handle them. "Like physical growth, psychological development does not follow an even course. It is marked by growth spurts, by periods of insight and reorganization, interspersed with rest periods of relative stability and self-maintenance."[16] Some get stuck with a certain world view and are too scared to give it up and face something unknown.

For our interests here, when children enter preschool, they already exhibit characteristics of their level of personality integration. At the third level, children manipulate others in order to get what they want. For that gambit to work, the child must be aware of rules governing social relationships. "He attempts to resolve the stresses of this phase by testing the limits of the rules and seeking for concrete and unchanging formulae which will enable him to handle all the problems that arise."[17] Much of the behavior is conforming, demanding, and instantly gratifying of needs. As the child likes clear-cut rules, it also resists changes.

At the next level of development, the child is more aware of the influence of others on her or him and their expectations. "He has accepted the impossibility of completely controlling or manipulating the rest of the world. . . . He tries to see himself as others will see him, attempting to predict their reactions toward him."[18] The child sees its identity alone and in relationship to others, is able to internalize, and can depict the roles of others: "the child now sees the *roles* of others as more or less discrete, disjunctive acts with little or no continuity."[19]

Still further along the scale, the child sees others and itself as more complicated and flexible, is aware of different points of view, can play different roles, can postpone gratification of desires, and begins to cope with feelings of discomfort.

> He has learned that it is possible to play the role of a father in order to handle a specific situation, but also that the role of a mother may be more appropriate in another situation. Within limits, he is able to shift from the role of a leader to that of a follower. . . . He can feel good about the happiness of other people, feeling good because he empathizes with them rather than because he has obtained power by being like them. As a result, he can enjoy people, can be stimulated by them, and can respond to them as individuals.[20]

As children's personality types are integrated at different levels, they can appear in children of any similar age. The classroom teacher is confronted with children who have all types and thus require different ways of learning.

In terms of peer teaching, the teacher needs to recognize the appearance of these traits in both the tutor and student. Such recognition can help the teacher to understand the importance of "matching" them as well as determining the choice of content. Students, at the third level, for example, will learn better with a tutor of a similar orientation. They will improve performance with instruction in more tangible subjects. Children who exhibit more intricate behavior, in contrast, need less structure and can undertake more flexible arrangements. These traits can be changed over time, but in the early phases of a project, teachers should understand them carefully. Often a manipulative child will merely learn another approach to maneuver people rather than change her or his way of relating.

LEARNING STYLES

Others speak of *learning styles*, *learning patterns*, or *learning orientations*. "Styles," writes Yale psychology professor Robert Sternberg, "are propensities rather than abilities: they are ways of directing the intellect that an individual finds comfortable."[21] "*Individuals can use more than one style, but they differ in their ability to switch among them.*"[22] "Education," he believes, "should foster students' ability to shift from one style to another as the situation warrants."[23]

Charles Schroeder defines the differences in the way students learn as *patterns*. From his perspective as a vice chancellor at the University of Missouri-Columbia, he has studied entire freshmen classes by using various inventories. He has discovered four general patterns which students exhibit on the instruments and in their classroom performance. He found that 60 percent of the students preferred a "sensing" mode of learning, characterized by:

> direct, concrete experiences; moderate to high degrees of structure; linear, sequential learning; and, often, a need to know why before doing something in general. . . the concrete, the practical, and the immediate. These students often lack confidence in their intellectual abilities and are uncomfortable with abstract ideas. They have difficulty with complex concepts and low tolerance for ambiguity. Furthermore, they are often less independent in thought and judgment and more dependent on the ideas of those in authority. They are also more dependent on immediate gratification and exhibit more difficulty with basic academic skills, such as reading and writing.[24]

These students have indicated they are in college to make money and have responsibility in administrative positions (up the corporate ladder). But he also finds this pattern of learning is characteristic of 75 percent of the general population.

In contrast, Chancellor Schroeder describes the remaining 40 percent of the students whose pattern is more intuitive:

> who prefer to focus their perceptions on imaginative possibilities rather than on concrete realities. Intuitives love the world of concepts, ideas, and abstractions. . . they often prefer open-ended instruction to that which is highly structured. They usually demonstrate a high degree of autonomy in their learning and value knowledge for its own sake. . . intuitives prefer diversity in ideas and learning options and are not uncomfortable with ambiguity.[25]

These students, he finds, are in college, "to become accomplished in the performing arts; contribute to scientific theory; develop a philosophy of life; write original works; or, create artistic works."[26]

Whether students consider themselves basically active (extroverted) or reflective (introverted) is another measure which influences students' learning patterns.[27] When Schroeder examined these characteristics with those of being concrete or abstract, he found that 50 percent of high school seniors were action, concrete learners and that 10 percent were more reflective, abstract learners. The remaining 40 percent were evenly distributed between the two types. College students were about the same proportionately. These learning patterns of high school students first showed up in their elementary years. The proportion of active, concrete learners in the public schools would likely be closer to the 75 percent he forecast for the general population.

Schroeder concludes the importance of his study is that many teachers interpret these "natural differences" in students as deficiencies. He speaks of the "mismatch" between what teachers prefer as learning patterns and what faces them in the classroom. At the college level, he found that three-fourths of the instructors preferred to teach the 10 percent of those students who had learning patterns similar to their own. Only 10 percent of the instructors preferred to teach the majority (60 percent) of students (those with action, concrete learning patterns). "[P]erhaps the greatest contributions we can make to student learning is recognizing and affirming the paths that are different from our own."[28]

Regarding the "mismatch" between teachers' and students' learning patterns, Professor Theodore Sarbin at the University of California, Santa Cruz, writes that:

> The teacher-pupil relationship is noncomplementary. . . . The pupil fails to grasp the operations of arithmetic, then, not because he is stupid, nor because the teacher is incompetent, but because of the confusions that arise when two parties engage in role behavior that is nonreciprocal. . . Such role confusions can be important background factors in a child's failure to learn in the traditional classroom situation. . . . In the past educators and psychologists attributed slow learning in the classroom to lack of aptitude or intellectual, motivational, or even neurological deficiency. In so doing, they have overlooked the fact that teaching and learning are activities carried on by persons in role relationships and that the roles constrain not only the instrumental acts of the participants but also the kinds of valuations (reinforcements) declared on the performance of such acts. Such ignoring of the social bases of classroom learning is witnessed by the stock treatment of "learning disabilities": the use of remedial classes.[29]

In terms of peer teaching, Professor Ann F. Mann at North Carolina State University has suggested the idea of "maps of development." This notion came from training college students as tutors for young children. Her conclusions are in harmony with those of the psychologists who developed the concept of integration levels. She found that

> [E]ffective tutoring is contingent on the quality of the relationship between the two parties. . . . Crucial to this development, [for tutors] however, was their capacity for understanding the interpersonal dimension of this role-taking experience and their capacity for resolving conflicts that arose during the experience. . . . Tutors' initial developmental levels may be less important than what they experience in this role and how they deal with those experiences. Tutoring often challenges tutors' preconceived notions about their peers and what it means to learn and to teach. The disequilibrium generated from assuming this new role could cause tutors to adopt less complex problem-solving approaches.[30]

With regard to training, she advises: "Tutor-training should focus more on individual differences and alternative problem-solving strategies. Training needs to include activities that will increase tutor' empathy and will help tutors learn how to respond to their students' fer

To summarize Professor Mann's "developmental n impact on peer teaching, I would see them as incre: *abilities*:

1. to understand multiple perspectives;
2. to distinguish between one's own and the tutee's f
3. to use more cognitively complex perspectives;
4. to recognize problems or conflict, experience the conflict, resolve it, and from it;
5. to be less dualistic and more accepting of differences: to be more flexible (seeing and using many approaches for teaching);
6. to use more individualized methods directly related to the particular needs of students (in contrast to generalized ones: repetition, review, asking questions, and the like);
7. to recognize and respond to nonverbal communication and behavior;
8. to develop a sense of competence in tutoring and in other areas of one's life;
9. to welcome and make a place for reflection.[32]

3

Getting Started: Nuts and Bolts

And gladly wolde he lerne, and gladly teche.

Chaucer

Successful peer teaching projects follow a systematic course of events which builds a foundation for teaching and learning. In the classroom, the practice begins with: (1) recruitment and selection of tutors and students, and redefining the teacher's role, (2) orientation and planning which includes assessment of learning and teaching styles, establishment of relationships, and the construction of a learner's profile, (3) means, methods, and content, and finally, (4) freeing up space—where and when to teach.

Most every student needs extra help at some point in learning—some more than others, some in different ways. And all classroom teachers need help. Some peer teaching programs begin with requests from teachers for children who have difficulties in specific subject areas (for example, reading or math). Older children who have mastered these areas, or those who are having similar trouble themselves, are a potentially helpful tutoring resource. Children may volunteer to tutor; or in some instances, teachers can assign them to help younger children; their own behavior may improve as well. Teachers, who are willing to give peer teachers more freedom, will allow them to select younger children they can help and to develop their own curriculum and ways of learning with the guidance and support of the teacher.

Help can run from remedial to enrichment; the only limitation is the teacher's imagination. Teaching can be on a one-to-one basis, one-to-two, and so on. Finally, it is good for the teacher to set a time limit for a project—an attainable goal. If the project is successful and the idea acceptable, a further project can be planned based on the experiences of the first, and so on.

Training consists of a combination of content, methods of teaching, and the practice of socialization skills in small tutorial groups. Tutors practice teaching one another in simulated teaching sessions with the assistance of role play and video.

RECRUITMENT AND SELECTION

We have a long history of "screening out" people who deviate from the mainstream. We label, intimidate, and isolate those who don't "fit." Peer teaching is the opposite; it works out ways for everyone to be included, to be successful, to develop their own uniqueness, and furthermore, it expands the perimeters of the traditional curriculum. Two university professors in Indianapolis, for example, did a survey of children who'd been placed in one special sixth-grade class. They weren't particularly interested in independent reading and were not among the high test scorers. But almost inadvertently, they showed enthusiasm to a question about their interest in reading to kindergartners. Taking the cue, the teachers helped the children develop a very exciting and creative program for the kindergartners; as no small fringe benefit, tutors' elective reading increased remarkably.

Recruitment and selection are intimately related. Some of the best peer teaching projects I've visited were those that were introduced quietly as part of classroom activities—simply as another way to learn along with the opportunity to help others. I've seen several launched with great flurry including logos, slogans, acronyms, certificates, and t-shirts. But such fanfare is not what it's all about. Children receive intrinsic incentives enough from their work and don't need what often amounts to demeaning tokens.

Tutors

There are no well-established, foolproof ways to select children to become peer teachers. (I have used the term *Teacher* to refer to the adult teacher involved in training, whether it be for the younger child or older one [the Lippitts refer to these as *sending* and *receiving* teachers]: *peer teacher* or *tutor*, and *student* or *tutee* for the children who are involved, and *trainee* for prospective peer teachers.) Some have thought, understandably, that their brightest students would make the best teachers; studies have found this assumption is not always true. Others believed the opposite, that "slow learners" could find the motivation to learn from teaching younger children with similar difficulties—a coupling in which both would benefit. In like fashion, still others have found that disruptive children might develop a new interest in school from teaching younger children, especially those who were just beginning to show restlessness or destructiveness. The belief was that if their image could change to that of helping someone, their disruptive behavior would become nonfunctional and simply disappear. It is no stretch of the imagination that all these suppositions *can* work, but all in all, perhaps the most important consideration is a child's desire to teach. Children can then acquire necessary teaching skills in short order.

In the beginning, some teachers find it useful to keep a distance of a few years between peer teacher and student, at least until everyone gains experience. If the gap between what is taught and learned decreases significantly, the peer teacher can become overwhelmed and discouraged. I've seen peer teachers who withheld information from their students when they were learning too fast (a practice not too unlike adult teachers).

Students

As for selecting those who need tutoring, there are two general guidelines. The first is for a teacher to select those children who need tutoring in specific subjects. These can be students who are having difficulties in learning content or those who have more general obstacles to learning, such as emotional, behavioral, or physical impairments.

The other rule of thumb is to involve the children from the beginning in the project. A teacher can ask who in the class would like some help with their studies; and, from the respondents, find older children who would like to help them. A variation is to let the peer teachers get to know children in another class, find out who they think needs help, and then decide if they have the proper skills to teach them. The latter choice is more risky of course, but can often produce some quite remarkable results both in terms of whom the peer teachers select and their unique methods of teaching. It begins a process whereby they are intimately engaged from the onset.

Perhaps the unfamiliar teacher might start with a more modest approach and, with experience, branch out. If one keeps in mind that all classroom teachers can use assistance in teaching, then one looks for their most pressing needs to begin a project. As one teacher put it, "I just said to the other teacher to send me some children who are slow, or who cause trouble, who are disruptive, or who you want to get rid of for a few hours each week. That was a way to get some children quickly without a long song-and-dance about what I was going to do."

ROLE OF THE TEACHER

I have used the term *teacher* here mainly to refer to the adult teacher involved in training and monitoring. The person doing the training can also be a counselor, psychologist, or other school personnel as well as someone from outside the school—a university professor, or some other facilitator. Teachers can make or break a cross-age program, wrote Peggy Lippitt.

> If you are a teacher of younger children you must consider the help of older students as a chance for your children to have individualized learning opportunities otherwise difficult to arrange. They should be appreciated partners. . . the role of the teacher is to support growth rather than maintain control. You become a promoter of collaboration, and establisher of norms of helpfulness rather than competition. You delegate responsibility and share the limelight.[1]

In another publication, Lippitt describes the attitudes of the "receiving teacher": "executives in charge of providing learning opportunities for their students. . . . They think of the older helpers as appreciated partners who can be links between the generations and explainers of facts and transmitters of values to the younger child. They share their ideas with olders and ask them for their suggestions and opinions."[2] In concert with these views are those of others: "The teacher becomes less the sole source of knowledge in the classroom and more of a manager of learning, an orchestrator, a resource person for both her own pupils and the children who teach. Similarly for the sending teacher attention must be given to integrating the teaching experiences of the pupils with their ongoing work.[3]

The role of the teacher then becomes one of:

- executive or manager who provides learning opportunities and delegates re-sponsibility for portions of teaching;

- partner, collaborator, linker: shares attention and ideas in teaching, learning; integrates teaching with learning;
- supporter of growth versus advocate of competition and maintaining control.

Part of the goal of planning and initial training is to help the trainees learn to recognize when they need help and know where they can get it. Teachers, as partners, can offer trainees certain teaching and content skills. They should always be available to give on-the-spot—or, in Peggy and Ronald Lippitt's terms, "at the elbow"—help; but not to intercede in the teaching session, thereby undermining the relationship between peer teacher and student. Such assistance, she believes, contributes to the confidence of the peer teacher, and at the same time serves a quality control function for the teacher.

The teacher's observations and suggestions are crucial for the on-going postteaching meetings. If the teacher has peer observers as part of the project, they may provide some immediate support merely by their presence. Observers need training so they will not take over the teaching situation in times of crisis. A teacher conducts training which includes the postgroup evaluation, which I will discuss in the next chapter. In the managerial role, the teacher shares that role with experienced tutors.

ORIENTATION AND PLANNING MEETINGS

"[O]ne can do training so as to retain and strengthen 'naturalness' as well as to squash it."[4] Before beginning a project, the teacher holds a series of two or three (or more) planning meetings for the peer teachers. The training group is formed with half a dozen or so trainees. The training can be short or more extensive.[5]

> It is our judgement that the pre-service training of tutors be short and not overly directive. It should deal with the question of who goes where, when, and what is expected of him. For some children this is all that is necessary for them to "give it a try," and they should be encouraged to do so. Others may want more orientation, perhaps including observation of the potential tutee's classes, role plays of tutoring sessions, and planning with each other or the teacher of the initial sessions.[6]

Regardless of their frequency, these meetings are concerned with building a relationship between tutor/teacher and tutor/student. Students learn how to identify the learning patterns or styles of the children and their own teaching styles. They learn the rudiments of what they are going to teach and the best ways to go about it. In addition to laying out details for the undertaking, these meetings set the tone for children to begin to see the teacher in a different light: as colleague, partner, and resource person in learning. The planning meeting will become absorbed into the project as the postteaching seminar—an integral part of the teaching-learning process and a self-study tool in itself. Social scientist Eric Trist spoke of the significance of planning:

> We are at the beginning of a new type of learning. Only through this will we become able to meet the faster, uneven, change-rate without losing coherence. Planning, which includes listening, is its master skill. A combined technocratic and democratic operation, it is a young and unmastered art, the new mold that its "culture" is beginning to "grow" in the post-industrial society. It is a process of unending imperfect co-ordination and of continuously learning more—about how to decide among seriously uncertain alternatives—so that some of the better features are kept open.[7]

Planning is not used in the rigid sense, but in a more dynamic one—a general strategy in which both student and teacher agree to try something new. Planning meetings also give an important sense of security—of teamwork—and become a reference from which peer teachers can draw strength and support during moments of crisis.

After a brief rundown on what the project is about, the first planning meeting might center around the peer teachers' getting to know themselves, and one another. What are their concerns, their hopes, and their peeves? The teacher might want to employ a brainstorming approach by having the trainees write down their characteristics on cards (which I'll describe shortly), and then discuss them as to their implications for their new job.

These traits form a base upon which to build a *relationship* between peer teacher and student—which begins with ways of getting to know their student. Such an assessment may include finding out their interests and their accomplishments, along with their failures and frustrations.

LEARNERS' PROFILES

Some trainees may believe that their own ways of learning are standard. In order not to impose their own learning styles on their students, they need to make an early estimate or assessment of the abilities and needs of their tutees. One way is for the teacher to ask the tutors to remember what it was like when they were the age of their students. Questions might be: "What is a seven-year-old girl like?" Or "Can you describe a six-year-old boy?" I've often used 5 x 8 inch cards for the trainees to list as many traits as they could think of (one trait per card, each trainee using a different colored, heavy felt-pen). In this brainstorming session, I attached the cards to a wall with masking tape, so they could be seen by the group as they were writing them. Although the cards were written anonymously, the different colors gave a visual representation of the participants and their ideas. Behavior traits ranged from anticipated characteristics—positive to prob-lematic. Distractions and keeping youngers' attention (fidgeting) usually came often, along with behavior traits such as shyness and aggressiveness. When there was about an average of five to six traits per student (prompting may be necessary to get some trainees shifting to a thinking mode), I next asked the trainees to help rearrange the cards into categories, a kind of scanning activity. Certain characteristics fit together; there will be sub-groups and others which overlap. Students can add new cards at any stage of the training session.

After we have decided the categories (they can be modified, eliminated, or new ones formed at any time), the group responds to their classification by critiquing the divisions. Some traits will be applicable to boys and girls alike, and some will be different. Consistencies, discrepancies, and ambi-guities present themselves.

Finally, the group will formulate an outline or mutually acceptable understanding of what their prospective students are likely to be. This base or foundation is corrective in the sense that it clarifies individual's fixed ideas and moves trainees toward shared or exchangeable ideas. The cards may be left on the wall to be revisited (rearranged, added to, or discarded) from time to time. Some children transfer the categories to computers or write them out to be duplicated for the others as a foreword to a "lesson plan."

This procedure gives trainees both a framework and a method for working together in a training group. The teacher's role is that of generating search questions. Children readily pick up the process and take charge of it. The use of cards helps to order conversation and move it from the ears to the eyes; it automatically cuts down on the need for only one trainee to speak at a time—everyone, in essence, can "speak" at once in an orderly fashion. No one's ideas are lost, even though some may be momentarily deferred.

In this way, we begin to assemble a profile (which can become a portfolio entry) of what the prospective peer teachers conceptualize students' behavior to be. We can use the same procedure to generate ideas about what the trainees found difficult or pleasurable recalling their own experiences at the age of their prospective student.

The profile can be helpful for trainees to use in identifying and maximizing their own teaching styles. From this profile, we can think out ways of teaching and learning as well as coping with anticipated difficulties. Which situations might cause peer teachers to become discouraged? What do they need help with?

Relationships also include the images younger children have of older ones, particularly those older boys who have a reputation for taking advantage of, or abusing, younger ones in the school, community, or at home.

In practice, sometimes tutors like to take their students outside the classroom for a walk so they can have more privacy and encourage the student to begin to talk freely. Children I have taught referred to these as "learning walks," which they used in their teaching from time to time to add variety and new experiences for learning. How to deepen this empathy between peer teacher and student can form the basis for future seminars in recognizing, describing, and shaping teaching methods to the individual learning style of the student.

Establishing a working relationship between the peer teacher and student, then, is the first consideration in training.

TEACHING STYLES

Having the trainees identify and develop their own styles of teaching is the next area for planning meetings. A card exercise is useful for the trainees to list their own skills and abilities, and what ways of teaching they think will be most effective for them. We can then categorize these and form the basis for identifying a variety of teaching methods. We can also identify areas in which they need further training. As many children begin teaching by mimicking teachers and adults, suppression and punishment are often the most common methods trainees use on their students. *"Given a chance to explore, to discover on their own, children tutoring will be less likely to mimic former teachers."*[8] Role playing is helpful in training sessions and can form the basis for group discussion as to the possible effects of their plans for teaching. Afterward, the teacher can ask for an alternative which can subsequently be role-played so the trainees can see different effects— adding other methods to their repertory.

If the teacher has selected the children who need assistance and the areas in which they need it, then these planning and training meetings can be more concrete and focus on specific methods of instruction. Through the relationship, however, the student identifies her or his own ways of teaching and learning. Often I have seen that as the relationship grew, the peer teacher discovered many things that were not apparent in the teacher-led classroom. Discoveries occur both in terms of special abilities as well as blocks to learning.

CONTENT, MEANS, AND METHODS

The third area in the planning meetings is an on-going assessment of the students' needs. Many teachers have particular students in mind for specific subjects like reading or math. Other teachers leave both the choice of whom to teach and the subject matter up to the peer teachers. They simply invite them into the classroom to find a child who needs help and then go to work. Regardless of the approach, part of the assessment is to pinpoint learning difficulties. Does the child have trouble with retention? Or does she or he have a short attention span?

Trainees should assemble a profile of their students' abilities and levels of learning beginning with their successes, before going into their problems. Questions can be used like: "What do you like most to do?" "What are you best in?" "What is easiest for you?" Then the peer teachers can move into the other areas by asking the student, "What is hard for you?" "What do you have the most difficulty with?" "What do you need help with the most?" And so, back to the cards—this time with their students.

If a teacher has selected twelve children who need special help with reading, then some training sessions on specific methods will be in order. But most older children already know these. The teacher can ask them how they learned a specific subject matter and, from their collective experiences, build a model for teaching specific content. Teaching materials inevitably follow. Peer teachers, with support and encouragement are extremely imaginative in devising them. Bill, the 12-year-old boy who taught with me, designed and constructed his own "learning kit" from wood. It contained an array of materials which he added to or discarded as he gained experience with the eight- and nine-year-old children he was teaching. He found he had to modify his kit as he began to move from teaching boys to girls and so on. He especially liked to take his students (he preferred to teach in pairs), out of the classroom, improvising wherever they ended up, bringing back materials and specimens for study in the classroom. And as we saw, these inevitably included "behavior specimens" as well.

Even when given the freedom to innovate, peer teachers often begin by imitating teachers in the methods they chose. Some arm themselves with books, papers, pencils, flash and drill cards and all the paraphernalia they have been exposed to without regard to their students' learning styles. Children who come from poor economic backgrounds and schools with fewer materials, often come up with more imaginative teaching methods. Simple devices such as fingers and toes for learning to count are often all they have. Later, homemade equipment, often very primitive, appears with the help of parents and siblings. Peer teachers should have an opportunity to experiment with materials as well as teaching methods. The postteaching critique is where they can evaluate and modify their methods of teaching. One of the most creative peer teaching projects I've seen was in a Head Start class where, at the beginning of the exercise, the teacher and peer teachers removed all the toys, games, books and so on from the room, leaving only a large oval rug and some cushions. They began by getting to know the children and establishing a relationship with them. And then they built their curriculum and added materials (many they constructed as part of the learning) as the project progressed; no content or paraphernalia was imposed on the children.

Regardless of the methods or materials, if teachers want to foster more creative learning, they must constantly raise the question: "Can you think of another way?"

Peer teachers get a good deal of comfort from anticipating situations in which they may have difficulties and then working out solutions in advance (which they may or may not actually use, but know they have them to fall back on). In planning sessions, the teacher might ask each prospective tutor to list three problems which might arise in teaching. Again, this procedure might be done on cards. When categorized and discussed, the peer teachers can list ways the problems can be addressed and then role-play some of the anticipated conflicts and alternatives.

To help build confidence, each trainee can then select the one area she or he is most anxious or unsure of from the array of envisioned difficulties and then concentrate on one or more ways to handle the situation when it arises. The teacher can help each trainee to develop three ways to cope with the obstacle. When trainees see that crisis situations can be turned into useful learning ones, a great deal of mastery and creative solutions occur.

Greater freedom from conventional teaching methods and authoritarian control by adult teachers inevitably brings about changes in the teaching situation; peer teacher and student test out new ways of relating and learning. Some peer teachers, as do adult teachers, resort to confinement and disciplinary measures to control the students. Or they give them "busywork." They need the opportunity to see the effects of their strategies, positively as well as negatively. Many of the crises in teaching happen when a student does not want to follow the plans of the peer teacher, or when she or he is under stress or restless. All these conditions are bound to appear early in a project. In the postsession they can reflect on what happened and role-play alternatives.

Before the first teaching session, it is useful to have the trainees pair off and practice teaching to one another. And then switch roles. This demonstration is done in the training group and the others offer their criticisms and ideas, which then can be role-played.

The following, for example, is an excerpt from a seminar in the early phases of twelve-year-old children teaching six year olds.

> Boy 1: I have a little girl and her name is Cathy and I teach math to her. She didn't do too well at first, but now she's getting up there. When she gets her work done, I take her out and let her play what she wants to for about five minutes and then she settles down and works good.
>
> Boy 2: Well, I have a little girl too and I let her do what she wants for a few minutes but then she starts messing around when I'm trying to teach her and then when I turn my back, she's gone.
>
> Boy 3: Well, maybe you can think up some jokes. I don't know any right off, but maybe you could make up some. There's a boy in our class who's pretty interested in math and he teaches. He gives the child jokes and this gets him interested in math.
>
> Boy 4: This might sound funny to you, but if she doesn't like to stay around, just sit her down and tell her how math came about. Jullian's tried it out and it works. Just tell her about the dinosaur or whales and when she's interested, then ask her what two plus two equals and then make up stories about that.
>
> Boy 5: Yea. Mark and Allen were in the room teaching their students science and when I wasn't looking, she left and went over to watch them.
>
> Boy 4: Maybe you and Mark and Allen could work together a little bit with math and science and maybe you could do some experiments in science and she might be more interested in you as a teacher that way. Because with science they discovered

math and if she knew that she'd probably say, "Well math is science" and then she'd have more interest in math.

JEANNETTE STOPS HER PEER TEACHING

As we all know, we can learn a lot from our mistakes. This excerpt from a class of mine highlights some of the traps that teachers can get into when moving too fast. These were teachers who were starting peer teaching projects. The vignette that follows also shows the importance of an on-going seminar for the teachers to share ideas and learn from one another.

When Dennie said that his teaching demonstration with children on Saturday might be a "complete fizzle," I thought about how my peer teaching *was* a complete fizzle. When I heard about peer teaching at our weekend workshop, I became a complete convert. I jumped in with both feet. Now, I'm one of the worst backsliders, because today I passed out this letter to my peer teachers which I hastily wrote this morning. I was unable to sleep much of the weekend trying to work this out.

Dear student teachers,
It has become necessary for me to discontinue the peer teaching project at this time. Perhaps it can be resumed at a later date. This has been an exciting and worthwhile experience for all of us and I'm sure that your interpersonal relationships with brothers and sisters and other first-graders has changed as a result of this. The teaching will probably continue in your own home or with friends, because you truly are teachers. Please accept our sincere thanks and appreciation for your dedication and enthusiasm and for the cooperation of your teachers.
Your friends, Mrs. W—and the boys and girls of room 10

Now this came about because last week one child very tentatively said in our "sharing time" meeting, "Could we not have teachers for a while and you be the teacher?" I asked what the others thought and heads were nodding and hands were waving. Some of their comments were: "We want more time for you to read to us." "Let the teachers rest for a while and get relaxed and then come back." "When some are absent and you have another teacher and then the first one comes back, they both want you and I feel bad." "Maybe if we don't have them come in for a while, we'll know which way we'll like it best." And then someone said, "A change is a good way to find out." My children were so much smarter than I was!

I was having a good experience as were the few being taught. The initial success was so good, I wanted to extend it. If a little seemed good, why not give it to all of them? I have a great difficulty in using moderation. So I had students coming in for half of their lunch hour, others coming at one, and still others at one thirty, so we had one-on-one teaching for the whole class.

This is where I made my mistake. It was a bit overwhelming to the students. At first there was some confusion and I just took the role of the teacher and said "Now this won't do. We're just going to have to do this more smoothly or we're going to have to call it off." Well, you know, they worked it out until it ran pretty smoothly.

But that wasn't the only thing I did wrong. I hadn't relinquished my role as a teacher of reading and math. I was doing that in the morning which took most of our time. The student teachers were to work on reading and listening skills. We weren't doing anything differently, it wasn't especially enriching, we were all doing the same thing.

In the first place, I didn't do enough pre-planning. I didn't have enough meetings with my teachers. Noons when I had planned meetings, I got yard duties, so couldn't even be in the room when they were teaching.

When I start it up again, it won't be on such a big scale. I'm going to have meetings with the teachers first—several meetings with children doing some role-playing so they can see how first graders learn and what they feel. First graders like to have routines and when they'd come in from the lunch hour, they were restless. I'd read a continuing story to them for 15 minutes until they calmed down. The peer teaching was taking up that time and they missed it. And then we need to talk about what things I'm going to teach, and what they will teach. I want them to do more things on their own initiative. We'll still be concentrating on reading and listening skills, at least at first. The children want more art and perhaps some of the sixth graders could think up projects for them.

Teacher 1. My children want the peer teachers to teach something different once in a while, so on Fridays, I let them decide what they want to teach. They work it out with their students; some want to continue reading, others write stories, some do music, art things, and so on. One sixth grader knows more about art than I could possibly give them. Friday is a fun day.

Teacher 2. (first grade). I have third and fourth graders come in for 15 minutes just before recess, to read to the children on a one-to-two ratio. They have their students sitting closely on each side of them. Some days the children take turns reading but everyone has a chance every day.

Teacher 3. I have fourth graders who come in every day and do reading with some of the children so I have time to take the slowest readers and work with them myself. I haven't started arithmetic, but soon.

Dennie. I was very excited when I visited Ellen's room last week. She had team teaching, peer teaching, with three different age groups going on all at the same time. I didn't see how she could manage so much at one time. But I've never seen so many children so highly involved with what they were doing.

Ellen. I found that reading and story telling was really a drain, and I don't feel nearly so tired with sixty children in the room as when I tried to help thirty with stories. I can tell you, it's not so strenuous.

Teacher 4. You must have spent a lot of time planning such a program.

Ellen. Well, yes, in the beginning I spent a lot of extra time, but it really pays off in the long run.

Teacher 5. I hear us talking about the fatigue factor in teaching. That's something I've become especially aware of this past week. My children [sixth graders] came back from Dottie's room [fourth grade] excited, but fatigued, really tired out. They were bubbling over, but when we got to p.e., they just dragged themselves through it. And in our seminar I said, "Something's wrong. What's the problem?" And they all said, "Teaching is hard work!" And that tells us something about ourselves. I was in the faculty room recently and talked with some other teachers and they asked, "How do you get free to do this [peer teaching]? And I said, "I'm resting. I'm tired. I'm fatigued! I've taught for 30 minutes and I'm bushed." And we were talking about teaching being a hard job. Maybe we just don't realize how tough it is and maybe that's why we give a lot of "filler" work during the day—just to give ourselves a rest.

CONSIDERATIONS OF TIME AND SPACE

The final area for planning is to determine when, where, and how long to teach. In the beginning, short teaching periods are best, lasting about 20 to 30 minutes. Establishing a time frame and holding to it enables children to experience some order and plan their activities accordingly. With experience and depending on the attention span of peer teacher and student, teaching sessions can be lengthened up to an hour, but there is no magical time span. Some children benefit from longer sessions, some from shorter ones. The main consideration is that both parties have a successful experience. Teaching sessions can be scheduled for two or three times per week, or they can be on a daily basis. They can take place during the regular school day, preceding it, on the lunch hour, or after school. Ideally they will become a part of the school day, as teachers give recognition of the importance in the curriculum that they deserve.

Children are ingenious at finding suitable places in which to teach. Even in crowded classrooms, they find nooks and corners where they maintain a certain amount of privacy in which to work. When a large number or a whole class is involved, the peer teachers can bring their own chairs and sit at the edge of the student's desk. When there is a difference of several years between the two, peer teachers sometimes exchange chairs with their students to make them feel bigger and thus not so overpowering.

In this planning group, sixth graders are discussing where to hold their teaching sessions.

Beth: Where can we go to do our peer teaching?

Shirley: Maybe we could take some tables out on the walk or in the corridor and work there.

Sue: I don't think we could work very well out there. People passing by would bother us.

Shirley: Maybe it wouldn't be so good. People might fall over us.

Beth: Not everyone would be working out there. Just those who wanted to work faster than the others.

George: Well, the ones that got finished first could help the slower ones. We don't all get through at the same time. That's what causes a lot of the noise and confusion in the room.

Outside the confines of the classroom, peer teachers find unusual places to engage in learning. Temporarily unoccupied areas like the cafeteria, the auditorium, the library, or the principal's outer office make good learning areas. The corridors outside the classroom can be used too, for a short session, if they are quiet. On one occasion, I donated my teacher's desk to the librarian as she needed an extra one; besides, I didn't want to be identified with a desk or have it come between myself and the children. The librarian, in turn, became interested in our project. Consequently, she voluntarily closed the library for one hour each day and made its space and facilities accessible for peer teaching, along with her assistance. For a few days the children found it strange to talk aloud and make noise in the room where previously only whispers were allowed. The principal also made her waiting room available during certain hours, an act which gave the procedure considerable status and made it visible to everyone. It also changed the expectations of the "outer office" being the place where students were waiting for disciplinary action.

Having peer teaching sessions more publicly exposed gives sanction to the procedure, clears up many of its mysteries and lessens the closed-door atmosphere of the teacher-led classroom. Visitors to the school can see individualized teaching and learning taking place.

Weather permitting, teaching can occur out of doors. In one school, the principal made a forbidden grass area a special one to be used only for peer teaching. A peer teacher in one of my classes held many of his short sessions on top of the parallel bars. He and his students found a certain amount of detachment at that height and he maintained that they had to concentrate harder up there; he was trying to "increase some of their attention spans."

There is always the objection that there is not enough time for peer teachers to be absent from their class and consequently they will fall behind in their own work. I know of no instance where this negligence has happened even when peer teachers were offering daily sessions. In fact, the opposite usually happens: with experience, most find that when children become peer teachers, they develop extra motivation for their own learning. Some teachers, however, select only those children who either need special attention in a given area or who are ahead of their class to become peer teachers.

Often peer teaching projects have to begin during the lunch hour, using half for teaching, the remainder for the postteaching seminar. Most children enjoy bringing their lunch and eating with their students or with the teacher. Often planning and training meetings are held after school when there is less pressure and fewer other children are about. One said to me it was fun to go home and—to his parent's disbelief—tell them that he had to stay after school; this time for a "teacher's meeting" rather than for something he had done wrong.

At first, most teachers maintain that their schedules are already too full. But when they see the value of the method and the enthusiasm of both peer teachers and students, they rearrange their priorities to give the project maximum conditions for success. With experience and acceptance of this method of teaching and learning, teachers and administrators usually will alter time and space to incorporate it into daily operations.

FINAL WORDS

It is helpful to ask each trainee at the last planning meeting to present her or his specific plans and rationale for the first teaching session. How to begin, what materials, if any, and where to get them? What help is needed? First meetings can be role-played usefully. The teacher can also ask the trainees to list three things (on cards) they expect to happen in their first teaching session, not specifying whether they are positive or whether they are possible difficulties. The training group can use these anticipated events for discussion. Some teachers duplicate them and during the first post-teaching session, give each participant a copy so they can compare their expectations with what actually happened.

Last, in spite of all I've said, better advice is not to plan to death. Many teachers in their conscientiousness (and compulsiveness) never allow for *spontaneity*—the great learning factor that takes place due to unforseen events and as a result of having fun. Peer teaching *is* different from classroom teaching by adults; children are both more sensitive to individual differences and more adaptable to changing conditions. After all is said and done, as one very successful teacher said in beginning a peer teaching project:

> You've just got to set a date and then jump in with both feet! When I finally got up the nerve to approach a first-grade teacher I thought might like to have some of my third graders help out, instead of the cautious reply I had expected, said, "Oh, that'd be wonderful!" And then when she started pressing me to begin and asking me questions in front of the other teachers, two, then three, immediately piped up and said, "Why don't you send me some too?" One was even the Head Start teacher. And then and there, without any warning, I had enough teaching jobs for all of my class. We had to work fast.

DIALOGUES WITH TEACHERS

There are naturally many questions about beginning peer teaching projects. The following are from experiences of teachers in the early stages in my classes.

Teacher 1. I took up the idea of peer teaching with my third-grade class and I hardly had to say another word they were so excited about it. We discussed how we might go about helping out in the first grade. One child asked what would they do if a child didn't want them for a teacher. A boy said you just give them a smack on the side of the head. Another said she'd just tell them once and that's all! And then one said, "You're just like my mother. She doesn't have any patience either!" My word, I was just stunned to see the images my children had—where did they get them except from adults? But later in our meeting, the same girl had changed her tune and said, "Well, maybe you could ask them a second time—but not a third!" I figured we had made a little progress. By the end of the meeting, everyone in the class volunteered to help out and they were beginning to discuss ways they could teach the first graders best and how they could still keep up with their own lessons. My biggest problem is that now the children want to spend their entire day doing nothing but teach!

Teacher 2. I began my peer teaching by getting some of my children together who seemed interested and telling them we were going to try something different by helping out in Ms. F—'s class. We didn't know what was going to happen, but no one could make a mistake and so there would be no failures, and we'd get together and talk about it afterwards. They had lots to talk about in that first meeting. We all sat there on the floor while munching our lunches. We discussed what had happened, how they felt about being a teacher, and then planned what they might do tomorrow. (They were teaching reading and arithmetic.) Later the teacher assigned us some students who were overactive and got into trouble—some she had been sending to the principal's office. And we got one very bright girl, who didn't want to do what the others were doing, like working in the workbooks. She had so much potential, but her teacher just didn't have the time to spend with her. It just grew from there.

Teacher 3. I have a very active boy in my fifth grade. I got him helping a first grader with numbers. He started with a math book but it was too advanced for her, so he began with building blocks. They got on the floor together and built some things. Then he taught her to count the number of blocks, and when she knew the total, he began taking one away at a time and helped her to figure out how many she had left. And then if he gave her more, what would the total be without recounting. He worked so patiently with her. Later he began to work with her on reading. But I'm afraid he got bored with the first-grade stories, so one day he came in with a copy of the *Reader's Digest*. I thought he was going to have her read, but instead, together they were going through the articles and picking out words they'd learned from her books. He soon got in over his head, as she began asking him questions about how the words were used in the articles. But the important thing was his interest and willingness to try different things. And she responded.

Teacher 4. I'm constantly impressed at how much children learn and can understand. And they don't shield anyone. I have this third grader who was tutoring a girl in the first grade. She wouldn't let him see her work— every time he tried, she covered it up. He tried so hard to help her and was so frustrated. He brought it into the seminar and the others went into all sorts of possible explanations until I thought it was getting out of hand. I would normally have reacted like the typical teacher and stepped in to stop the cross-examination or at least guide it into something more constructive. But you know, they worked this all out themselves. Someone had overheard the girl say, "I don't care. I'm not going back to copying." And that seemed to give the group the clue they were hunting for. She had been copying other children's work, and her teacher wanted her to work on her own. But she felt it wasn't good enough for him. I thought their conclusions were just marvelous—and remember, they are only eight years old! They could figure out how Ruthie felt and even one boy, who at first wanted to dismiss the whole thing, was right in there trying to figure out how to help. You just don't give young children credit for having this kind of understanding— we don't give them the chance.

Teacher 5. One of my students was to teach a little girl and she wouldn't talk to him for the first whole half-hour. He wanted to teach her addition and he tried everything he could think of including using his fingers, but she just turned away. In our evaluation meeting the others gave him a lot of ideas. Some of the other teachers thought he needed some teaching materials, and so, in my enthusiasm, I went out and got a whole pile of stuff for his next teaching session. Well, it didn't work: she still wouldn't talk and yet she'd been listening all the time, for she brought him some additions she had done on her own. And they were all right! He was so excited, he could hardly wait for the teachers' meeting to tell what happened. And she now began to look him right in the eye. What did I learn? You have to ply your way slowly and not interfere!

Teacher 6. I have one boy in my class who had trouble with reading, but he was good at math and liked p.e. activities, but he was so disturbed all the time, I sent him to see the psychologist, who told me the child was so upset emotionally that even traditional counseling wouldn't help him. I didn't know what to do, so I asked him if he'd like to be a teacher. He seemed interested and has been working at it faithfully and has settled down a little. Now he's asked for help from an upper grader with his reading.

Teacher 7. I had one interesting response from a parent. George was not doing well at all, he was so far behind the others and didn't have any interest. He was so far behind in algebra that he couldn't possibly catch up in the 12 remaining weeks. I had sent three notices to his parents but of course got no reply. Then I thought about making him a teacher in the lower grades. Well, he went home and told his parents and his mother was on the phone the next day. She wanted to know what this was all about—he'd asked her for help in order to teach and was so enthusiastic. And he'd told her that he was so far behind in math, he couldn't get caught up before the year was over. She was demanding that *he* also be tutored, and that as a teacher, I ought to be challenged by this! Can you imagine?

4

Teaching and Reviewing

Because we enjoy each other's company, we generally learn best from each other.

Mark Stefik

Nothing succeeds like success. After peer teacher and student have established a relationship, each should have a satisfying experience. Teaching is best begun in small manageable morsels, bits that can be completed in a single lesson. And then after this initial encounter, the peer teacher can undertake more ambitious tasks. A teacher is available to offer support, but remains unobtrusive during the teaching session. Some are effective, others are not. But the avowed teacher will often gain a rare and valuable insight into the nature and effectiveness of her or his own teaching methods.

Following the teaching session, the teacher meets with the peer teachers in a tutorial to review their experience. What went over well and what went wrong? What different ways of teaching could have been more effective? The teacher offers expertise on teaching and observing, and in so doing, forms a new relationship with the peer teachers—that of colleague or mentor. The new role is often in sharp contrast to the authoritarian one of the traditional teacher.

Peer teaching should get off to a good start. Teachers, peer teachers, and students alike should have an initial successful experience. As each approach will vary greatly due to different methods, attitudes and beliefs, no one way works best for all. But there are certain common characteristics: the basic pattern is planning, teaching, assessment, and revision. The director of a project training college students (North Carolina State University), found that: "Tutor training programs. . . need to provide beginning tutors with a great deal of support, to spell out the limitations of the tutor's role, to discuss the dynamic and interactive nature of learning, and to define student success as broader than just earning high grades."[1] Tutors who seemed to benefit least from tutoring, "may have ignored feelings because of their preoccupation with assessing the success of tutoring sessions."[2]

In the early phases, while gaining experience and feeling one's way, it is wise to keep the teaching sessions brief and oriented toward short-term goals: a time frame or completion of a task. Twenty to thirty minutes is often as long as some children can remain attentive at the beginning. "It is important that the first learning task be easy enough to ensure that the tutee can perform well, since initial learning strongly affects the tutor's attributions about the tutee's ability, liking of the tutee, and reaction to tutoring another child. We know from other research that a teacher's expectations about a student can influence learning."[3]

After establishing a relationship with the student, peer teachers may select one skill or simplified concept to teach in a single session. Many peer teachers in their initial enthusiasm have a tendency to overwhelm students with content. They soon learn in the postteaching critiques how better to estimate the student's level and style of learning and adjust their approach accordingly. This form might resemble "microteaching" (a cyclical process of teaching, critiquing, and reteaching) which has been used successfully at all levels—nursery school through university—and in all areas of content.[4] The teacher, an observer, a tape recorder, or video can be used to monitor a tutoring session. In the postteaching seminar, the peer teacher has the opportunity to review her or his teaching immediately with the help of the teacher and the other tutors. Modifications may be in order for the next teaching session. The tutor thus has a safe place to learn and practice basic teaching skills. One minimizes the potential for microteaching when teachers apply the concept routinely and unimaginatively, not allowing the tutors to expand. In time, nonetheless, many projects become student-centered as the peer teachers become secure in the relationship and skilled in teaching.

As for content and methods, teachers who want to learn the most from peer teaching projects must be willing to set aside many of their preconceptions: we simply do not know enough about effective teaching to be closed-minded.

The Developmental Studies Center in Oakland, California, has produced a comprehensive approach to peer teaching in their "Buddy" program. It combines learning with developing relationships among elementary school age children.[5] Teachers are encouraged to work in pairs with two teams collaborating. The far-reaching program is built on four basic principles: (1) Relationships, which "foster a sense of community and promote personal relationships that are warm and supportive." (2) Values, which "include social and ethical learning as an integral part of the Buddies program." (3) Open-ended Learning, which uses "open-ended activities to engage students at their own level of challenge and to give them fair and equal opportunities to learn." (4) Autonomy and Responsibility, which "routinely give students opportunities to exercise autonomy and responsibility."[6]

To carry out these exemplary goals, the project staff include ways to prepare both peer teachers and younger children to sustain academic learning and build supportive relationships. When the "Buddies" have been matched and an orientation has taken place, the older child begins plans to compile a "Buddy portrait." The profile begins with an interview which may include talking about things of interest to the younger child: cherished objects, favorite books, things the child does well, and so on. The interview can be supplemented with drawings the couple initiate, with dolls or puppets, improvised scripts, and socializing. Both students are encouraged to keep "Buddy journals" which can become part of their portfolios, and to maintain contact by "B-mail." Teaching is not confined to the classroom, but can occur on field trips, walks, eating together, and from home visits. Larger scale activities include projects in the community (a "green team" to promote ecological awareness) and volunteering ("working for a cause"). The basic method of planning, action, and reflection is given careful attention with guides to its implementation.

CLASSWIDE PEER TEACHING

We normally associate peer teaching as older students teaching younger ones, but children can also teach and learn from each other in the same classroom. Some teachers pair up children who have mastered certain skills with those who have not. The procedure remains essentially the same as with cross-age teaching: planning, teaching, and review. In some instances, teachers hold the review session with the entire class participating which enlarges the opportunities for learning. In Kansas City, Kansas, researchers conducted a large-scale classwide peer teaching program involving 10,000 students and 516 teachers, in the elementary grades of forty-two schools. They found, over twelve years, that students were "able to learn more in less time. . . compared with conventional forms of teacher-mediated, teacher-led instruction."[7] Furthermore, when these children reached middle and high school, they showed "higher achievement, lower special education, and lowered risk of dropping out."[8]

Two teachers in Oakland, California, teamed up with a teacher training professor in a nearby university and initiated a remarkable cross-age multicultural reading program. They were located in a year-round elementary school of more than 1,300 pupils, many of whom were learning English as a second language. Fifth and sixth graders became "Buddy" tutors for a first- and second-grade class.

Each of the two teachers held a ten-minute preparation ("minilesson") before the teaching session. These lessons dealt with "procedural issues," "reading and writing strategies," and "social, interactional, and management issues." Over a course of ten minilessons, the tutors, as well as their students learned basic tutoring skills and how to make the most use of their allotted time. The teachers included role-play in the lessons. During the teaching, the teachers offered "one-on-one coaching," or "at-the-elbow" help. Following teaching, each teacher held a "debriefing" session. Children took 10 to 15 minutes to write up what had transpired (which might include their drawings), and then the teachers got them together for a classwide discussion.[9]

In another school, how one whole class taught another is illustrated in the example that follows.

There was a bustling about as thirty children and their teacher took their chairs to the combination first- and second-grade classroom. They were to spend the next half hour assisting the teacher in giving a lesson. She began by putting six words on the blackboard and asking the children to make sentences using those words. The exercise was both to understand the meanings of the words and to spell correctly. The fourth graders were to assist the younger children on a one-to-one basis. The older children were seated beside their student. Some were looking on as their student wrote the sentences, while others tried taking dictation from the younger child. And others were trying both.

One older girl was having difficulty with her student, a small red-headed boy, who happened to be her cousin. He wrote a sentence about *her*. I was sitting near by (as an observer) and he asked me how to spell the word he'd written ("stupeed"). She cautioned me not to give him help, so he turned to some of the other fourth graders.

I noticed Ramon who was helping a boy. At one point, he put his arm around the child. I pointed out to the teacher the importance of Ramon's example: the importance of touch as a way to establish a positive relationship. The librarian was visiting the room to take photos of the children;

she overheard my remark and took a photo. Ramon immediately withdrew his arm and some of the other boys from his class snickered. The time was up and the first-grade teacher called the two classes of sixty children together to hear some of their sentences which she put on the blackboard for all to see.

After the session, the fourth-grade teacher took her thirty children to hold their critique outside on the lawn under the trees (as it was a very hot day). The children complained that the photo-op was a distraction. The students said that it had been difficult enough to hold the younger children's attention. Some peer teachers were concentrating more on posing for the photo session than on their student.

I asked Ramon how he felt when the boys laughed at him. He was embarrassed. Some of those who'd giggled said that you weren't supposed to put your arm around another boy. The teacher and I were amazed how children, at this early age, had developed ideas about "politically correct" expressions of male-to-male behavior. When I asked Ramon if he liked his student, he replied, "not especially," but he wanted him to know that he was there to help him. He added that in a previous teaching session, he'd disciplined a student who wasn't paying attention and said how bad he felt about this afterwards. So he was trying a different way with another student. I followed up by saying that Ramon was the boy's teacher, that he'd done well to get the boy's attention, and I thought they'd had a good teaching session.

The girl, who was trying to teach her cousin, said how difficult it was to hold *her* student's attention and asked the group what she could have done. Someone said you should never attempt to teach a relative or another child that you were close to outside of school; it would interfere with the teacher-student relationship. Another child agreed and said simply that in the future, she should select a student she didn't know. Period. Again, I was amazed to see how these children had picked up adult values and were applying them. The group tried to think out alternatives. One suggested that others could have assisted her as a kind of neutral back-up and to support her in the teaching situation. Another recommended that she have an assistant so there wouldn't be so much stress on her alone.

Someone made a comment that everyone seemed so serious and there wasn't much fun during the session. Others said that more effort should have gone into making the session not seem so hard for the students. Some thought the tutors could have given more attention to making the youngers feel good, to feeling big, and having some fun. On the latter suggestion, one suggested that if they reversed the setting and brought the children to *their* room in the future, they might feel bigger. Or, if that was not possible, at least they could exchange chairs and let the student sit in the larger chair. That way, the students would be sitting a little higher and the level of communication would be more equal. And the tutors didn't think they had enough time to get to know the students or to encourage them to think about how to use the words. Some wanted to go on and make stories out of the words.

The teacher brought the children's suggestions to the first-grade teacher and so they agreed to have another session where the children would come to the fourth-grade class to concentrate on reading.

REVIEW AND CRITIQUE

This account of one peer teaching session among two total classes highlights the importance of reviewing the meeting. In the span of only a few minutes, we saw an array of topics and behaviors that were fundamental in teaching and learning. The tutors were sensitive to the atmosphere and how they could make it more conducive to learning. They had ideas about *teaching methods* and their *effects*—and how to improve them. They were concerned about behavior, both their students' and their own. They revealed attitudes and values which could be examined. The first-grade teacher was apparently impressed enough by their tutoring efforts to invite them to do some more teaching on their own turf.

An integral part of successful peer teaching is the postteaching seminar. It should follow the teaching sessions as soon as possible when recall and emotions are high. This meeting is a time for pooling experiences and ideas and learning from one another through live encounters. It serves an ongoing training function for evaluating learning and teaching and for making plans for future sessions. Taping these sessions is often helpful for instant playback or later review by the tutors and the teacher. Videotaping is an even more powerful tool for learning. Having observers is another. Any means used to increase objectivity and accuracy of recall will improve teaching.

The seminar can begin with the teacher's inviting the participants to give a very short resume or account of the teaching sessions. After a brief general run-down from each tutor, the teacher may ask: "Who would like some help with their teaching?" During the discussion, the teacher has an opportunity to add observations made during the teaching session. If peer observers are used, now is the time for their contributions. (Chapter 5 discusses the role of peer observers.) If the peer teacher has taped the teaching session, then very short excerpts may be useful.

Teaching often arouses considerable anxiety—anxiety which the teacher can use constructively for growth if dealt with properly and while still fresh. Often a peer teacher has had a crisis which will automatically take precedence. Teachers habitually have the tendency to step in to salvage a stressful situation, thereby undermining the peer teacher. In the postgroup, after a peer teacher's frustrating experience, a teacher's mere comment about the subject's difficulty will start things going. Simple questions will stimulate discussion: Who else has had a similar experience? What have others done?; or Can you think of another way you could have tried? If the group gives support skillfully and at the right time, they strengthen the role of the peer teacher and often new ideas spring forth. When they have discussed the situation to everyone's satisfaction, the participants often put forward practical suggestions as to other ways to try out.

Teachers draw on their knowledge of teaching and display their observation skills to help peer teachers become more observant and proficient. They should deal with successes in the same manner (but not necessarily be rewarded) so that peer teachers can maximize them.

They should avoid judgments, especially what is right and wrong; rather, they can develop a more constructive framework around the question of *what happened* and what was the *effect?* Turning problems into challenges is one of the tasks for the teacher. An important part of that task, once more, is striving toward objectivity and neutralizing moral stances. When peer teachers are relieved of these issues, they learn to evaluate their own performance constantly—and to try something different, if not satisfied.

The evaluation meeting, then, is where the greatest amount of overall learning and change occurs. A teacher, "liberated from the rote task of supplying information—a machine can do that. . . can be a partner in learning and dedicate himself to giving his pupils the necessary criteria to judge their data's integrity, make connections between different facts, and formulate opinions and arguments of their own."[10]

Patience and belief that peer teachers can work things out are essential, something akin to Rousseau's aphorism that when raising children we have to learn how to gain time by losing it.

The following excerpts are from a series of postteaching seminars which focus on the importance of dealing with the peer teachers' behavior as it affects the teaching situation. These ten- and eleven-year-old children discuss a very trying session with six and seven year olds. The passages focus on some of the training problems and the kinds of help peer teachers need. They also underscore the value which spontaneity can provide.

John volunteered to include Bill, the student of another peer teacher who was to be absent for the week, with his own. (John had become a tutor as his teacher had thought the experience would help him control his overactivity in his classroom. John, to everyone's surprise, took to tutoring and became very serious about his work. He had done quite well teaching on a one-to-one basis.)

> John: Bill cheats. Well, today the teacher's in there and he's there workin' and every time I turned around to go help my own student, well, Bill would just run and play around an' everythin.' An' so then, I asked him real kindly if he'll sit down an' do work a little bit and he kept on hollarin'. I never had trouble like this before—an' he just kept on hollarin'! I gave him five pages of math an' so he done it an' then when I leave he goes and tells somebody else that he can go through the pages and then do anythin' he wants to or feels like doin'.

John revealed his concern for his student along with his own image as a teacher in the eyes of the other peer teachers and with the students. Only a few weeks previously, the class saw John as irresponsible and the root of a lot of the trouble in his classroom, a reputation he brought with him from the previous year. He showed his frustration and need for assistance in coping with his student's behavior:

> I tried this mornin'. He got back up an' started hollarin' again an' wanted to talk to somebody else who was tryin' to study. I just got hold of him and spanked him. And then he settled down. So, I left him alone. Well, he was real good after that little spankin'—he settled down then. If he keeps actin' up like that I keep tellin' him, "I'm gonna tell your teacher." He say, "Please don't tell my teacher." So, I tell him, "You either gonna act right or I'm gonna' tell her." And so he say, "Okay!"

John asked the others in the seminar if it was alright that he had spanked his student, as he was feeling a little guilty. This turn of events was encouraging, for heretofore he'd never admitted that he needed help or allowed the others to question his tactics. Previously he'd not shown any awareness of his inadequacies or the effects of his boisterous and aggressive behavior on others. The other peer teachers understood his frustration and, while not condoning the spanking, urged him to try other ways. In a few days, he came to the seminar with these results:

I decided that I should work with him more than I do right now. Instead of helpin' everybody else, I'm gonna work with him a lot now. When he's readin', he can't pronounce most of the words. So what do you think I should do?

Joe: Give him a couple more swats and he'll sit still and pronounce the words!

John: No. I don't think that would do any good. I think if I can get somebody to help me work with him, he'll probably be a little bit better. I think if someone a little smarter could help me, like Claudette, she's higher'n her grades an' everythin', so I think I should get her to help me with this little boy. What do you say, Claudette?

Claudette: It's okay with me.

Furthermore, John, in his solution, dealt with both cross-racial and cross-sexual issues. Both John and his student were black, Claudette was Caucasian.

I give still another example of a postteaching seminar: this time a total passage because it illustrates how inventive children can be in adapting to a new situation. It's also a good illustration of a teacher's ability to let the children work things out. The teacher participated only at the beginning and at the end. The meeting follows the first session of fourth graders (nine and ten year olds) teaching second graders (seven and eight year olds). Many of them were Native Americans living in semipoverty conditions on a reservation on the edge of the desert in southern California.

Ms. B, the second-grade teacher had asked Ms. C, the fourth-grade teacher—a student of mine—for remedial help with some of her students. Furthermore, she asked Ms. C if she could send them to Ms. C's room in order to use the time they would be away, to teach another lesson to those who remained. Ms. C (who had considerable experience with peer teaching and classroom discussion groups) decided to have the postgroup meeting for the peer teachers in the presence of the rest of the class, a total of about forty children. They had witnessed the tutoring and the teacher thought all of her pupils could benefit from the discussion.

Teacher: We've had an unusual experience this afternoon by having second-graders in our room to teach them reading and I'd like to hear about your experiences.

Boy 1: The boy I had was sort of shy but I think that the reason was because that we're a lot older than he was. He kinda got nervous and that's why he missed a lot of words.

Girl 1: The boy I had was around seven and he missed five words, but he sounded them out for himself. After he read the story, I asked him the words again and he knew them right off. I think he was a pretty good reader.

Boy 2: The two boys I had, well, one missed a lot of the words and the other one hardly missed any because he was a real good reader and I thought so myself but he kept on saying other words, putting other words in the story. I think he's going to be a pretty good reader when he grows up.

Girl 2: Would you like to have him again?

Response: Oh, yea.

Girl 2: What did you learn from it?

Response: Well, you have to have patience.

Boy 3: Did you like your student?

Response: Yes.

Boy 3: Did he pay attention?

Response: Yes.

Girl 2: Did he like you?

Response: I don't know.

Boy 3: Was he snotty or did he call you names?

Response: No, he didn't.

Girl 3: The little boy I had was very nice. He missed a few words on the page but he sounded them out. He knew the story. I asked him a few questions about the story and he knew them. He was very nice and I'd like to work with him for a lot of days.

Boy 4: Did he pay attention?

Response: Well, sometimes he didn't.

Girl 4: The girl I had was real good at reading and the only thing was that she didn't keep her mind on was what she was reading.

Girl 2: How did you help her?

Response: Well, I just told her to keep on reading.

Girl 2: Did she like you?

Response: Yes, I think so.

Girl 2: Did you like her?

Response: Yes.

Girl 5: The girl that I had talked so low I could hardly understand her. When she didn't know a word, she would make one up or she would talk so low I couldn't hear her, or she wouldn't say anything. And I couldn't understand her, so the words she didn't know, I'd write on the board and by the time I'd got that done, she'd be on the next page.

Girl 3: What did you do about her not talking loud enough?

Response: Well, I tried to get her to talk louder but it didn't help.

Boy 2: Was she very shy?

Response: Yes.

Boy 3: I think the reason they didn't quite want to work or something was because we're fourth-graders and they're only in second grade and we want to rush through everything. They can't read that good and they want to go slower and read the words that they can so they can learn something.

Girl 6: The student I had read alright, but she kept her head down in the book and she kinda talked low. I learned that you have to have patience with them because some of them don't want to mind you and they want to do something else or they want to read and they want to talk real low.

Boy 5: The student I had, well, he was kinda nervous because he knew I wanted to rush through some of this stuff and sometimes when he didn't know a word and I tried to help him with it he just didn't want to learn and well, he got kinda, I don't know to explain it, he got kinda upset because I knew all these words and he didn't and he was so nervous that he was fidgety.

Girl 7: Well, the boy I had, I learned from him that I think they always want to learn. If they want to learn they really try so I think you have to have a lot of patience too and give them the chance sometimes to be off by themselves to read and then they understand more words.

Boy 6: The girl I had, I knew that she wanted to learn yet she didn't know the words and so I learned that you have to have patience and not rush them.

Girl 3: I learned that you have to be real patient with them because they are not all alike"— they're different. With mine, she wanted to learn, but I kept wanting to rush her and I kept wanting to say, "Hurry up and read," but I didn't.

Boy 7: I was sitting with Peter and his student. Pete's student missed a lot of words but Pete wrote them down for him on a piece of paper and he made him figure out the words and...

Girl 3 [interrupts]: What did you learn from this?

Response: Well, I learned that Pete knows how to teach the guy; he can make him learn the words by writing them down and making him say them over and over again.

Boy 8: At the same time when I was with my student, I was kinda watchin' the others. They were reading alright, but they were looking around and the people would have to get them back on the track every time they'd do something that they weren't supposed to and they wouldn't work. Well, they'd get them back on the right track.

Girl 4: I learned that if you had an advantage like we had to teach somebody, just see what it's like and not try to rush through it so they can go back to their room.

Boy 4: It's not very easy to teach second graders. They don't like to sit still and write for a very long time.

Teacher: Well, I guess you all agree that you need to have more patience with little children.

Children, when given the freedom to explore ways of teaching, will often come up with novel practices, combining various methods, as one peer teacher observed of another:

> I feel that the effective method that Linda [tutor] used was allowing Jeanne to become the teacher and she became Jeanne's pupil. Linda would purposefully make mistakes when Jeanne was using the word flash cards with her. In this way, Jeanne would have to correct her and tell her the right answers, proving that Jeanne knew the correct answers as well. It had become very monotonous for Linda to continually quiz Jeanne of the flash cards. The most important technique that Linda used with Jeanne was to present her with her own problems and let Jeanne try to cope with them. Again and again, I noticed Linda ask Jeanne if she could play with crayons or draw or go outside and play. Each time that Linda would do this, Jeanne would look somewhat annoyed but she would always think of something better and more constructive for Linda to do. Later I noticed

that Jeanne was less inclined to ask Linda to let her color so much. After suffering the same problem herself, she finally realized Linda's problem and tried to help her with it.[11]

The postteaching seminar is where peer teachers can experience simple, yet quite far-reaching, changes in attitude and behavior. Children need to be released from already fixed attitudes, as we saw earlier in the chapter when Ramon experimented physically with ways to reinforce learning. Relationships cross generation gaps as they do with genders and races.

DIALOGUES WITH TEACHERS

Question. I can see how girls would take to peer teaching, since so many of their teachers are women, and it may just be a natural "instinct" for them. But what about boys? Wouldn't they see this as something only a "sissy" would do?

Answer. That's what a lot of teachers believe, but I've seen many examples of how boys get involved, especially in the sixth grade—around twelve years old. They love teaching, worry about their students and are constantly thinking up new ways to teach so it won't become boring or too difficult. And it can have rather profound effects on their own behavior—positively.

Question. How does peer teaching work with children teaching others of the opposite sex? Is it as readily accepted as children teaching the same sex?

Answer. Although some teachers prefer to match children of the same sex, I've found that it doesn't matter; in fact using children of the opposite sex often gives opportunities to examine a broader range of social behavior.

I had a shy, rather demure eight-year-old girl in one of my classes with whom I just couldn't seem to communicate. She always looked so frightened of me. I asked a sixth-grade boy if he would help her with reading and told him of my difficulty. He wisely took time to try to get acquainted with her first. In the postgroup discussion he said that she was getting uneasy, and that perhaps he was going too fast for her. He seemed a little discouraged, and he asked the others if they had any ideas of how he could make her feel good. The other peer teachers asked him what kinds of things the little girl liked to do and he said play hopscotch. He'd actually gone onto the playground with her so she could teach him the game. He'd watched and had her describe how to play the game, hoping to find a way to get involved with numbers. I asked him if he played hopscotch with her, and the others laughed. When I asked why they laughed, someone explained that boys don't play hopscotch with girls: "That's a girl's game!" "But you are *her teacher*," I replied. Nothing more was said. The next day in the seminar, he reported that he felt that he'd been able to make a good relationship with his student; he'd entered into the game with her, and not one of the boys had teased him about it. That simple juxtaposition clarified roles for him, which freed him to enter into a successful relationship with her to the benefit of both.

By coincidence, a few days later, I'd invited some of my students to visit the class. An observer reported that one of the boys had put his arm around his first-grade student while he was teaching. The others laughed and someone made the insinuation that he might be gay. One of the boys spoke up and said: "He's *his teacher*." Immediately everyone understood. The teachers later told me how shocked they were that the forbidden area of homosexuality could come up so openly and that the children could handle it so well. Well, children are observant, and they absorb a vast amount of information from a great number of sources. Furthermore, they put it all together, make their own interpretations, and act accordingly. And sometimes they're wrong.

This was a "living-learning" situation where so much happened in such a short time. It could be the beginning of these children learning to question many of the sexual stereotypes they had acquired, and even sexuality itself, if we were brave enough to face it. There are unlimited side-effects if teachers are willing to take some risks and not be so bound up with preconceptions. And you have to overcome the fifty reasons why you can't try something different!

Question. Children in my class are reluctant to teach a child of the opposite sex. How could I encourage them to try?

Answer. As they become more secure in their roles, you could raise it in the postteaching group at an appropriate moment. Or you might use a crisis-situation to introduce the idea. One day, a peer teacher, who was teaching a child of the same sex (girls), was absent. I asked a boy if he could fill in and he responded without even thinking about it. Later, he reported what a good experience this was; he was glad that he could help me out. But it was a new experience for him to teach a younger girl.

Or you could find a child who needed help and say to a peer teacher, "She needs help and I think *you* could help her." It's not a matter of same or opposite sex, it's the *relationship* that matters. Do you see? It's also the spontaneity and seizing the "teachable moment" to implement changes.

I once saw an aggressive twelve-year-old boy—one of the bullies of the playground—get assigned to teach a six-year-old girl. As he was getting acquainted with her, she quite casually took hold of his hand on the playground in view of all the others. This was a crisis moment for him, and he had to make a decision on the spot. Was he going to change his whole image in the eyes of his "gang" to keep holding her hand? Or would he revert to his previous destructive image with the other guys? Through such a simple interchange, incredible growth opportunities are possible.

Question. What happened?

Answer. He stood his ground and continued with his "lesson." I didn't hear of any repercussions from his peers. But you notice how important it is that you build a *new* peer group. If you begin with five or six peer teachers, you have the nucleus of a training group that establishes its own values and expectations. Then when you set up a second training group, or take in more to your first one, the power of that group increases. They can handle much of the negative peer pressure coming from the outside.

Question. I'm confused about the observers. Where do you get them and how do you work with them?

Answer. The idea was evolutionary. A group of sixth graders had been teaching throughout the year. Later in the spring, they began to get bored as their students had progressed and didn't seem to need them any longer. They were looking for something to do and someone suggested that they could help train the newer peer teachers. One idea was that they could sit in with them in their teaching sessions, make notes and then furnish their observations in the postgroup seminar. We gave them some basics on how to observe and record and then they went to work. At first, they tended to be too assertive; in crisis situations or when they saw a peer teacher make mistakes, would step in to correct the situation. But they soon found that intervention undermined the position of the peer teacher. With some role-playing sessions, and from their own teaching experience, they became skilled at observing and got a great deal of satisfaction by adding a more objective element to the program. They developed systematic ways to observe—especially nonverbal behavior. They wrote summaries and worked up their findings into graphs and charts. Some used tape recordings and, when we began using videotape, they became quite skilled at recording. Eventually a few began to refer to themselves as researchers. I brought some of them to the university campus to help me teach teachers how to observe. It was their own doing—evolving from applying what they'd learned to other areas—starting with their own teaching, moving on to observing, then to researching, and finally, to training new peer teachers. Others found satisfaction in continuing their teaching, working with the same students in different areas, or taking on new ones. The flexibility to experiment accompanied with the right kind of support and skill training is so important. Have any of you had any similar experience?

Teacher. I divided my class into peer teachers and observers—one-on-one. I met with the observers and we talked about what we would be looking for as being a kind of second-eyes-and-ears for the tutors. I found that I had no training in observing or experience with that kind of notetaking, so we just all learned together. They soon noticed the irregularities between what the tutors said and how they looked, all the little signs of tension and so on. And gestures, how some used their hands to reinforce what they said, the nods of approval or the scowls. The children caught on fast and it became kind of a game to see who could spot the most.

Teacher. I had an unusual situation with an eight-year-old Asian refugee child, who had only been here one-and-a-half years and spoke little English, but was very perceptive. We had more volunteers to do teaching than we had students at the time and so I had discussed the possibility that some of them might become observers and report back to the seminar what they saw and heard. I was surprised a few days later in the group when I asked for observations, and Pam waved her hand enthusiastically. She stood up and produced a paper on which she'd been keeping notes, and in her broken speech read off her observations.

Question How do you handle peer pressure that children experience when they talk openly about another that might be seen as "tattling?"

Answer. It takes time to change the culture of the class—the attitudes and values, and the expectations the children come with. Again, it comes by building a new culture in which children see that open communication is not dangerous and that the teacher is a partner rather than an enemy. That they can safely share their observations when given openly and honestly. I guess some of the sociologists would put it in terms of "role rehearsal" where children need opportunities to try out new behavior before adopting it wholeheartedly. That begins in the safety of the training group and is amplified in the postteaching seminars. But I can give you some thoughts of fifth graders:

Teacher: What's the difference between helping someone and tattling on them?

James: Well, if you ask them why they do something in the group meeting and try to show them the right way, it will help them.

Sally: When you tattle on someone, you have a good feeling inside. But when you give feedback, you feel bad, because you might lose a friend—for a while.

Visitor [teacher]: What about using letters to tell what has happened about people and then no one will get his or her feelings hurt. Or we could say, "I saw three people doing this," and not mention names. The people we were talking about would know who we meant, but the group wouldn't. The problem would be solved too.

Jim [to the teacher]: Are we going to start to use letters and no names?

Teacher: What do you think about that?

Jim: I think it's better to say the name. Then we know who to help.

James: I agree. Maybe we could get away with something without the group finding out about it. But then we'd never change.

Sally: Anyway, I don't think anyone gets too embarrassed for long over things we bring up here. It's the truth, anyhow.

5

Keeping Track: Effects and Evaluation

Kids are our test sample—our advance scouts. They are, already, the thing that we must become.

Douglas Rushkoff

There are, as you would expect, enormous side-effects from peer teaching. Mastery of teaching and success in the relationship brings spontaneous growth in both peer teacher and student. It strengthens and makes smoother transitions from childhood to adolescence to early adulthood. It transforms troublesome behavior into constructive behavior. It changes relationships of children with adults, particularly teachers and parents, as well as with older siblings. It transforms teachers into partners who benefit from each others' endeavors. Perhaps its most fundamental purpose is to insure that "all children are successful school learners."[1]

In order to better understand the *what* and *how* of peer teaching, some form of systematic assessment is needed. Evaluation should be built into every program and preferably become an integral part of the exchange. Children learn the importance of, and participate in their own, assessment. Ideally, evaluation is self-correcting: to "inform instruction." It tells what the student knows in terms of designing subsequent learning activities.

You cannot set up an effective peer teaching program by defining for the teacher or tutors precisely what procedures they must follow or what attitudes they must have. Aside from clearly stated goals, assumptions, and strategies, there is the less tangible element of integrity, which cannot be acquired by command. But as the late ethnologist, Gregory Bateson, said, it can be transmitted. "The minimum requirement . . . is affective integrity and a belief that this integrity will permit the identification of self in others. With [these characteristics] probably any individual automatically helps." Replication of programs, he continued, "hinges upon finding leaders with these very general and not too rare characteristics."[2]

Habits are hard to break, even when we know they no longer work for us. Evaluation is an essential part of the way we do things and a better way to know where we are going, how things are standing at any given moment, and what is better than mere hunches and guesses to chart our futures. The argument is that we can improve upon these natural, often intuitive, actions.

How does one evaluate change? There are those who are obsessed with standardized tests. To satisfy *their* needs, one can give them. But as Brenda S. Engel, who was on the graduate faculty of Lesley College (Cambridge, Massachusetts) for twenty years wrote: "The primary purpose of judgmental assessment, which relies on standardized testing, is to sort and evaluate students. This kind of testing contributes little information useful for instruction."[3] Test scores, as we all know, have serious limitations. They don't tell the whole truth or give the whole picture. Test scores can be misleading as many competent children have blocks to uniform testing. And they can have repercussions. In the end, success in any area is measured by accomplishments, not by test scores. But in education, we seem to be mired down by such scores. I say "we" but, in reality, it seems to be politicians, the media, and some education administrators who are so preoccupied. "The primary task of assessment," Engel continues, "is to inform instruction: To explore and define what the student knows and can do in order to plan further learning."[4]

A number of years ago, a student of mine began a small short-term project involving a half dozen of his sixth graders; by year's end, his entire class of thirty-five children were tutoring in the lower grades on a daily basis. The following year, as the class moved on to junior high, six of the boys returned to tell their former teacher of their disappointment and boredom. They missed tutoring, so the teacher proposed that they return to their former class and teach their underlings. Together they decided they would teach math. The tutors each took about six students to teach as a group. They did an assessment on each of their students, which included math achievement along with learning styles. Then they proceeded to teach. The tutors couldn't have time off so they had to scurry over on their lunch breaks two times each week. They met with their former teacher after school twice a week for a review. To keep track of their undertakings, the principal administered a standardized math test. Just before the Christmas recess, the principal retested the thirty-five sixth graders. To her surprise, math test scores for the class as a whole had jumped the equivalent of two grades; even the lowest had accomplished all that was required for the entire year.

Now, they had to face the realities of our lock-step education: If they continued teaching math, what difficulties would their contributions impose for the sixth graders the following year when they moved on to the next grade?[5]

As a method, peer teaching appears to be a forceful tool. Researchers at Stanford compared the effectiveness of four learning strategies as measured by standardized tests in math and reading. They found cross-age tutoring was more effective than computer-assisted instruction, reduced classroom size, or increased instructional time by adult teachers. Furthermore, cross-age tutoring was nearly four times more cost-effective than reducing class size or increasing instructional time.[6]

But more important are the qualitative changes in learning that can be demonstrated much more effectively by some form of portfolio assessment. Engle says: "Authentic assessment, associated with meaning-based pedagogies, implies assessment practices that contribute directly to classroom instruction and to education."[7] She distinguishes between short-term assessment for expediency (standardized testing) and a long-term view which accepts children wherever and whoever they are. "Education," she wrote, "should be an opportunity, not an imposition."[8]

What evaluation *should* accomplish, then, is a corrective function that is built into learning at every phase—not pitting one child or one class against some hypothetical norm—so that evaluation actually becomes a part of learning. Instead of a summation of the past, each person constantly evaluates her or his own progress oriented toward the future. A peer tutor and student, for example, can assess where the student is in terms of a particular subject area. Then they establish their own unique goals, as tentative as they might be at the moment. They decide how to achieve success (what they will need and what obstacles may stand in their way) and how to chart their progress as a team. They take frequent samplings of what they've accomplished that will enable them to use assessment when it's appropriate. And so the observations become a rectifying instrument, rather than one of reward or punishment for any given result. The peer teaching project in Texas took the competitive element out of its program by turning it inward. Each tutor with her or his student devised a numerical system in which "the partners would lose points for every word the first grader misspelled and for every word the fourth grader checked incorrectly. Each team tried to beat their last week's score."9

In plain terms, evaluation is merely a way of bringing together systematically gathered information and then using it. Most teachers say they are "doers," and don't understand or need research. That's fair enough, but that assumption only means they do or do not get away with having to check on their own effectiveness. I once heard a young, ambitious principal, upon taking office, say that his school was there to improve the children's learning (he meant in terms of test scores). He was a man of action and wanted the word out that he was in charge, that things would get done, and that he didn't have time to study what the school was doing. He wanted "results." But he didn't understand that "doing" *implies* study: you can't simply *do* some things and not learn. So, it's not a matter of learning *or* doing; they are inseparable. Rather, it's the organized, systematic and, effective gathering of information, making the necessary program decisions, carrying them out, and then asking further relevant questions. This cycle is one that makes us professionals. And children can be taught this procedure early in life.

None of us can function without information: rumors, hunches, and inside tips from family members, children, or people we work with. And we get a vast amount of information from the media: newspapers, magazines, journals, books, radio, television, and the Internet. We are constantly bombarded with information—some useful, some vague, some distressing, some inaccurate, some contradictory. Somehow we must sift through it all and use what's helpful to us in making day-to-day decisions. Some information is immediately applicable, such as a new procedure that seems likely to work. Other information is stored away, hopefully for future use. Most is forgotten.

So each of us has a living computer inside us, an immense storehouse of information, and we are continually adding to that fund. We are also our own programmers; we constantly draw upon this spacious data bank to help us make practical decisions in our work and personal lives. It's not limited to adults—children are constantly asking piercing questions to get information and are evaluating the helpfulness of our answers.

Evaluation has a certain logical sequence and a few basic methods that, if used more systematically, can improve our own effectiveness and that of our work. To begin with, we need to know as clearly as possible the beliefs or principles under which we operate. For those who practice peer teaching, the first belief is that children (and adults as well) can learn from one another as well as teach one another. The degree to which peer teachers and students (the consumers) share that commitment will determine the effectiveness of the program. The consistency and skill in converting one's belief into daily practice will affect the amount of satisfaction the consumer feels. So, in a sense, all of us are evaluators, constantly assessing what we do and, as consumers, what we receive. If we are at all sensitive and responsive, we try to improve our efforts. We ask ourselves: Is there a better way to offer our services? Or, as a consumer we ask: How can we get the assistance we need to be more effective in our work? Answers to these questions may then lead to changes.

This process of evaluation also serves as a management tool: (1) to recognize clearly our operating principles, (2) to check on their implementation (quality control), and (3) to have a record of our results. Results, in turn, may lead to further questions and modification. Evaluation then begins anew in a cyclical, on-going process rather than simply as an assessment of a static result.

PROGRAM DEVELOPMENT

Six students and their adviser at the Far West High School in Oakland, California, worked out a basic way to evaluate programs. They adapted a method from research and development procedures used in industry; a six-step procedure beginning with a work team.

1. Make sure that everyone in the group is able to discuss problems without being afraid of feeling stupid or being embarrassed. Encourage others to share their ideas. Look at all angles of the program from as many points of view as possible. Keep an open mind. Don't burn out. Don't give up on your goals or objectives. Don't cop out. Don't take the easy way out. **Be a winning team.**

2. Discover the needs: Find out if what you want to do is really important. A **need** might be a problem that must be solved or it might be a lack of something. There are certain things you have to know in order to find out if your program is really necessary. A program that seems like a very good idea to a group of people might be totally unnecessary. Don't just come up with a list of problems. Figure out what are the causes of the problems and then plan a program to deal with the causes. Don't take on more than you can handle.

3. Set goals and objectives: Brainstorm to set general goals and specific objectives. The **goal** of your program is what you are generally trying to accomplish. The **objectives** are more specific and include the date when you think they should be finished. **Goals** and **objectives** are set up to meet the **needs** your program was set up to deal with. Before thinking about *how* to get where you're going, you will first have to know *where* you're going.

"Would you tell me, please, which way I ought to go from here?" Alice [*Alice in Wonderland*] asks the Cat.

"That depends a good deal on where you want to go," says the Cat.

"I don't much care where. . . " says Alice.

"Then it doesn't matter which way you go," answers the Cat. Once you decide where you are going and what your **goals** and **objectives** are, the rest of **program development** will help you get there.

4. Look at the force field: The **force field** is made up of everything that might affect your program. Try to change anything that hurts your program into something helpful. The forces that help your program can be strengthened. And sometimes you can even change the forces to improve your program. The three things you always have to consider are what's happening to the program, what's helping the program, and what's getting in the way of the program. Looking at the **force field** gives you a more complete picture of the problems and needs that you must try to meet. **May the force (field) be with you!**

5. Plan strategies: Be flexible enough to change your strategies when necessary. **Strategies** are plans to meet your **goals** and **objectives**. Some **strategies** are *inside* your group and some are activities *outside* your group. Remember that all **strategies** work within your **force field**. If your main **strategy** doesn't work, don't give up! You can always change your **strategy**. As a matter of fact, as a starter, you should make up several **strategies** in case one doesn't work out. Always try to make the *inside* and *outside* **strategies** work together.

6. Integrate feedback: Be open to feedback and use it in your program. **Feedback** is all the information, comments, ideas and criticisms that come from your program and can bring about changes that will improve your program. There are two kinds of **feedback**. The first is your group's own comments, ideas, and criticisms about what they are doing. The other kind is made up of information and statistics gathered outside your group. When looking at **feedback**, you must ask these questions: (1) Is your program reaching its objectives? (2) Should you change any of the specific objectives or general goals? (3) Are your strategies working? (4) Should any of the strategies be changed a little bit? (5) Should you drop any strategies and replace them with new ones? (6) Has anything happened to your program that you weren't expecting? and (7) Is your program meeting the needs it's trying to meet? Another important use of **feedback** is to prove to people in your **force field** that your program is working and deserves their support. No matter how successful your program seems to be, you must check it out carefully. In order to do this, think about these four things: (1) What things are making the program successful? (2) What things are

happening that you did not expect? (3) What other groups are being affected by your program? In what ways? and (4) How long does your group think these effects will last? Now that your group has gathered **feedback**, you must **integrate** it. Integration means using this information to strengthen or change each of your **objectives** and **strategies**. **Feedback** might eventually tell you that your original goals should be changed.[10]

COMMITMENTS

Another way that teachers can use assessment in learning is to have tutors and their students make short-term commitments or predictions of what they want to accomplish. Students can make commitments individually, as pairs (tutors and students), or as teams (tutors, students, or both). Such pledges can be done on a daily and weekly basis. Their projections should include a time frame. Students can record these "statements of intentions" and then note what actually happened. Whether the goals were achieved on time or there were discrepancies, the results form the basis for discussion, analysis, and subsequent action. Sometimes it's just as revealing to analyze why a forecast worked as predicted as to why one failed. "This expected-to-observed feature is the heart of the systematic self-study process. Individuals and groups have implicit personal-social theories, frames of reference, or integrations for understanding the interpersonal and task relationships with which they must cope. Man is very good at avoiding changes to his ways of understanding which can force changes in his ways of perceiving."[11]

PEER TEACHERS' PROGRESS NOTES

Teachers in some projects have used still another means of qualitative assessment—peer teachers' journals or progress notes on their students—in postgroup reviews and for further training. They could see changes in behavior as well as content learning through these observations. For example, twelve sixth graders at a small rural school of about 200 students, kept track of their students' progress as well as their own observations on themselves in their entries:

John (a first grader) is taught by Jim. At first, John showed very slow improvement and was being forced to do everything by Jim. Jim had to make him sit down, sit still, and force him to do things. Slowly, John started learning as Jim became more aware of his different learning style. As they progressed, John showed rather remarkable progress and seemed to want even more outside work to do. His teacher reported that, in a few weeks, he had moved from the bottom of his class in reading to the upper one-third. Perhaps the main thing is that someone showed a little interest in John and this was something nobody had ever done before. His whole attitude toward learning has notably changed and he wants to get down to business immediately when the teacher begins. He has recently asked if he could become a teacher also, asking if he could teach a kindergartner everyday as Jim works with him.

Bill is the most task-oriented of the twelve peer teachers. During a 20–minute teaching session, he is very much "on edge" and is serious toward learning. He is the most consistent of all the peer teachers. Daily he gets down to work and shows a strong interest in his teaching, although in the teaching seminar afterward, he's very critical of his teaching methods. I believe that he is a little threatened because of Lucy, his current student, who is very strong, aggressive, and a fast learner. She puts great demands on him and is very willing to learn. He's beginning to look at her attitudes now rather than just teaching, causing a great change in him.

Mary is very impatient—impatient with anyone she works with. She's especially bright and is having difficulties with her student. Her student doesn't want to settle down and doesn't seem interested in learning which makes it hard for Mary to find a role for herself.

Robin is very consistent, always tries hard, and gets to work even when her teaching doesn't go as well as it could. In only two weeks, she's shown considerable improvement as she becomes more patient with her student. And she's getting along better with adults; she now has questions about her student that she needs help with. She's also having serious problems at home which is interfering with school.

Paul was the least interested in teaching. He just didn't seem to be able to settle down and be serious. He tried, but needed continual pressure to keep working at it. But in the past few days, he seems to be working with less pressure and showing more interest since his student is working with a kindergartner. Paul's taking on a new role in helping his student with problems with *his* student, and now seems very enthusiastic. His attitude has changed in just a few days.

Sally is extremely dependable and is an excellent teacher. She is teaching two children. She plans her lessons well and immediately goes to work. She's very quiet, dependable and sturdy in her relationship. At first she was very slow until she caught on, but now spends a great deal of time outside class preparing her lessons. She has a lot of trouble in the seminar with the other peer teachers—sometimes she's loud and hard to get along with. But her success in teaching seems to have given her something to hold on to and now she's more able to look at her own behavior in the seminars. She's made one of the biggest changes of anyone in the group.

Lucy's the strongest of all the first-grade students. She is most serious about school work and, although she is very shy and never talks to strangers, she likes being taught by a peer teacher. Last Friday, I took her down to the kindergarten because she wanted to become a teacher. She has two different learning styles. On the one hand, she likes being shown how to do things, and on the other hand, she wants to do things on her own. She's an active learner and wants to keep busy all the time.

ASSESSMENT BY PORTFOLIO

I learned the importance of extrapolating from life experiences as a faculty member when I was evaluating men who were incarcerated and wanted academic credits. This training was at an experimental university; the appraisal was in the field of criminal justice. On one hand, I was teaching courses to students who were learning about the field theoretically, but for the most part had no direct experience. On the other hand, I was evaluating portfolios of offenders who had a wealth of experience, but knew little about theoretical issues. The prisoners had assembled impressive dossiers of their life experiences in crime, which essentially was a work history. The prisoners included copies of their arrest records, court proceedings, testimonials from crime partners as well as victims and family members, tape recordings, and photographs. One even included a "scrapbook" he'd kept of newspaper clips reporting his criminal activity for many years, and indeed it was prolific. Some had completed correspondence courses and a few had been able to take college extension courses while confined. Experience though, abundant as it may be, is not enough. From their accumulations, I had to determine what they had learned about things such as the functioning of the justice system, the "causes" of crime, how delinquency can be altered and prevented, the social organization of communities and prisons, the effects of punishment, and so on, then offer advice on what studies they needed to supplement their rich experiences to better understand and communicate their knowledge. Indeed, had their experiences contributed more than information about their work histories? Then, I had to make recommendations as to where and how they could augment their backgrounds. So one of the important functions of the prisoners' portfolios was to bridge experience with theory.[12]

Likewise, children of all ages, even though they may be lacking in years, have fertile backgrounds upon which they can draw. When they enter a peer teaching program, tutors can learn how to keep records of what they've learned and what they produced: work samples from all the various areas of the curriculum. Not unlike college students in teacher training, peer tutors can assemble a portfolio that they consider portrays their skills in teaching and can caption their entries with their reflections. When children begin to assemble (ideally beginning in preschool) and then update their portfolios, the process becomes a learning one in itself. "The ability to think about what one does and why, and assessing of past actions, current situations, and intended outcomes, is vital to intelligent practice—practice that is reflective rather than routine."[13] Students develop new skills—those of organizing, reflecting, and understanding their experiences. "When students begin to make decisions about the way in which they organize portfolios, they begin to reflect on and develop understanding of their professional roles and responsibilities."[14] The experience can form the basis for lifetime learning. Had I been aware of the many uses of portfolios early in my teaching career, I could have better assisted the mother who asked me for a recommendation for her daughter who wanted to pursue peer teaching. A dossier of her daughter's accomplishments would have said far more than my letter.

In the same manner, tutees can keep track of what they've learned from the experience and how they have been able to apply their skills and learning. These cumulative records also give children a better basis for determining what they need, and want, to learn. "Student portfolios," claim two teacher training professors, "provide a mechanism for students to become reflective independent learners, and portfolio development encourages teachers to facilitate individual processes."[15]

Brenda Engel suggests four general areas for consideration to demonstrate student accomplishment in learning: (1) skills (handwriting, word spacing, numbers, facts, etc.); (2) student's control over information; (3) higher-level skills and understanding; and (4) personal characteristics and habits of mind (curiosity, inventiveness, willingness to take risks, self-confidence, sociability, etc.).[16]

Deborah Meier has developed a "habits of mind" framework at Central Park East schools in Harlem. The school itself, she writes, "is a reminder of the power of reasoning, assessing, revising, and planning."[17] Furthermore, she continues:

> We refuse to let our work be judged on the basis of a student's capacity to collect trivia. We want it to be judged instead on the intellectual habits of mind it engenders. And we also value certain habits of work: the acceptance of increasing levels of

responsibility, the increasing capacity to communicate appropriately to others, a willingness to take a stand as well as a willingness to change one's mind, and being someone who can be counted on to meet deadlines as well as keep one's word.[18]

In shoring up these ever-evolving "habits," the teachers ask questions of themselves simply: "the question of evidence, or 'How do we know what we know?'; the question of viewpoint in all its multiplicity, or 'Who's speaking?'; the search for connections and patterns, or 'How might things have been different?'; and finally, why any of it matters, or 'Who cares?'."[19]

Portfolio assessment has replaced standardized testing at Central Park East in its elementary, junior, and senior high schools. "Students," Ms. Meier maintains, "should be expected to demonstrate their abilities directly—to 'show' what they know and can do. Multiple-choice tests are not a substitute for the real performance."[20] Students begin to assemble a portfolio over the years that will track their progress in seven areas.

Another imaginative and commanding tool akin to the portfolio is that of *student exhibition* of accomplishments over the years. A high school in Missouri has initiated the practice of students' demonstrating their proficiencies in the areas of personal responsibility, critical thinking, writing, public speaking, and multimedia presentation. Each student has a three-member advisory committee composed of a randomly assigned teacher and two others, which the student selects: one from the school, and the other can be from the community. The student submits plans to her or his committee for the presentation; they meet from time to time to assess materials the student is developing and set a time line. The presentation is open to the public and there are no grades. The exercise is rated by the committee as (1) distinguished performance, (2) proficient, (3) proficient with reservations, or (4) not proficient. The latter rating is temporary and implies that the student will revise the presentation. The practice has had unexpected side effects: "what began as a simple inquiry into assessment has grown into an enriching educational experience for all concerned. . . a unique opportunity for faculty members from different disciplines to confer about student progress. . . people who now work collaboratively in ways they seldom did before."[21] The authors also note, "a new sense of community around academic achievement" and "new relationships between our school and our community."[22] In not such an extensive approach, I've had peer teachers do demonstrations of their work for teachers, parents, and administrators in my university extension classes, both live and on television.

Some years ago Fort Pitt Elementary School, located in a poverty-ridden neighborhood in Pittsburgh, initiated an *Independent Research Project* among its students. One week each month, groups of ten fourth and fifth graders with a teacher become a research team to study a self-selected topic. College students who are in teacher training join them in planning, teaching and evaluating their project. "Each day they get to work alone or with one or two classmates, to work as part of the project team, and to engage in community outreach activities—going on field trips, hearing guest speakers, or making presentations to peers or parents."[23] Part of applying their research activities is helping out children from the lower grades. The project is built on a number of assumptions:

- Children learn most rapidly in a community of learners.
- Children do not have to learn basic skills before they think critically.
- Learning is more meaningful when it is integrated.
- Families and community are an indispensable part of learning. [24]

From their projects, the children apply their research skills in classes during the other three weeks. "Teachers now incorporate some project strategies into regular instruction. And the role of the teacher has changed from dispenser of knowledge to resource person."[25]

CHILDREN AS OBSERVERS AND RESEARCHERS

Teaching is mostly listening and learning is mostly telling.
Deborah Meier

The celebrated former principal of Central Park East Elementary and Secondary School in New York's Harlem can make that statement from her many years of teaching, administrating, and from the benefit of a higher education. Furthermore, people will listen to her. But a group of sixth graders in one of my student's classes came to a similar conclusion after a year of peer teaching and observing other tutors at work and from observing their teachers over the years. They had become concerned about defining effective teaching practices. Now they wanted to check out some of their hunches. A brief training session was held to help them learn some observation skills. They did some simulation exercises by pairing off, one teaching a lesson to another, with a second team observing. The observers compared their observations for accuracy and then

practiced some more. They soon learned to separate opinions and interpretations from observations (what you can *see* and *hear*). Then they were
matched with peer teachers in their classroom. Their observations were
included in the postteaching seminar in an effort to aid its objectivity.
They reported their observations to the total class:

Boy 1: I observed Eric giving his student words he already knew and then
he'd slip in new ones. When his student didn't know a word, they break it
up by letters and try to figure out the meanings together. And I think that's
a good way to learn, to teach.

Girl 1: How could you see or hear that last statement you just made?

Boy 1: Well, it seemed that way to me.

Girl 1: But that's only your *opinion*. You don't have any observations for
that.

Boy 2: Joe was teaching Jimmy by putting his words back to him, like
when he'd give him a definition of a word or ask him a question about one,
Joe would say, "I don't know, could it?" His student likes to read—you could
tell by the smile on his face.

Girl 2: I observed Sally give her two students a test—and this is my
opinion—that Sally was favoring Carolyn because when she gave the right
word, Carolyn would show it but not when the other girl did. She puts one
student up and the other down.

Boy 3: How did she show it?

Girl 2: Carolyn always smiles when her student does well. I think that
shows she likes her.

Girl 3 [to Carolyn]: How much do you like her?

Carolyn: A lot.

Boy 3: How much is "a lot?"

Carolyn: Well, I like her most of the time.

Boy 4: I think Carolyn is too caught up in giving tests. George also is
giving his student tests. It's all beginning to look like a contest.

Carolyn: Well, how can you know if they learn if you don't give tests?

Boy 4 [continues]: I don't like the whole idea of giving tests. It puts the
student down. Myself, I get real embarrassed to see this going on. I just
don't like it.

Boy 5: I don't think it's necessary, period!

Teacher: Well, then how do you know if your student is learning? Is this where the observers' data could help us?

Boy 6: I have an idea—if you have two students, they could be more like a team than in competition, and help correct each other.

Boy 7: I don't like it when the observer interrupts. He teaches while he observes.

Boy 8: When you told him to stop, did he stop?

Boy 7 (responds): Yea.

Observer: Well, it's hard being an observer when you see the teacher doing something wrong, or when he misses something and he does it all the time.

Boy 8: *All* the time?

[Observer]: Lots of times.

Boy 8 [continues]: Well, what are your feelings when he does that?

[Observer]: I feel kind of dumb.

Girl 1: Would you rather teach than observe?

[Observer]: No, I don't think so.

Girl 1 [continues]: Well, then how can you teach and observe at the same time?

Boy 8: Don't you think he was trying to help you by knocking down how you were teaching?

Boy 7: I wasn't complaining about that—he took over teaching my student and I want to teach him by myself!

Girl 1: Why don't you just tell him not to interrupt?

Boy 7: I do, but he keeps on asking my student questions.

Observer [responds]: I wasn't doing the teaching, I was just showing him something he'd missed.

Teacher: Evidently there are some things you're doing that you aren't aware of how it's effecting the teaching. Do any of you have any ideas of what this might tell us?

Girl 1: It depends a lot on *what* you're doing.

RESEARCHERS

In time, the children had more discussions about what constituted good teaching and recalled traits from personal experiences with their adult teachers. They actually formulated an overall hypothesis that the teacher should talk less than the student. They also wanted to learn more about the range of attention span of students in order to individualize lesson plans. So, in order to check out their assumptions, they decided to concentrate on studying the nature of the interaction between peer teacher and student. A college student helped them work out a way to identify and tabulate the "units" of talk each initiated and thus compile a profile for a given session. Their expectation was that, if their hunches were proven and if tutors were given this feedback, they would "correct" their methods and become less talkative.[26] They role-played teaching sessions, calculated their observations, and checked among themselves for reliability.

Equipped with clipboards and stopwatches, they began to study the interaction between peer teachers and students. Much like quantum physicists, they were mindful of the effects their observations would have on the teaching-learning process, but found out minimizing that "nuisance variable" was difficult in practice. They began to share their observations with the total class.

Teacher [in a postteaching seminar]: You know how *you* like to be taught, how much you like to have teachers talk to you, and how much you like to talk. Now that you're the teacher, is there anything here that will tell you what you're doing?

Girl 1: You find out if the peer teacher is acting like an adult teacher who talks a lot and so you can find out if the student teacher is trying to copy his own teachers and not let his student talk very much.

Teacher: Is there anything that the researchers could give us some help with?

Boy 1: I was researching Tim and his student was watching me. Tim gave out fifty-three message units in the first 5 minutes and twenty in the second 5 minutes; yesterday he gave out twenty-five in the first half and thirty-five in the second half.

Boy 2: I researched Jim. Yesterday he gave out 39 messages, today 34. His student had 35 units yesterday and today he had 45. His students' total attention span yesterday was 6 minutes and 44 seconds; today his total attention span was 8 minutes and 20 seconds and he didn't talk as much either.

Teacher: So his attention span increased about 2 minutes today compared with yesterday? Anybody else have that kind of result?

Observer: Rodney was teaching his student math problems. Yesterday he had 4 minutes and 58 seconds for the first half and 5 minutes in the second half.

Teacher: So there wasn't much difference?

Boy 3 [to teacher]: I don't see how these unit messages are going to help us. Could you explain a little bit?

Researcher: Well, this is what they talk about, when they give out a complete idea, I mark down one.

Boy 3 [continues]: But is that supposed to be helping us by writing down how many units? I don't get it.

Researcher [continues]: Well, we're trying to find out if the teacher talks more than the student. . .

Girl 2: Can you speak up?

Researcher [continues]: If the teacher gets carried off on a trip.

Teacher: Maybe the researchers don't understand what they're doing. I thought they did, but Pete didn't seem to be able to explain it when asked. And furthermore, it seems to be upsetting to some of the teachers and students. Maybe it's just a waste of time.

Pete: It tells us something about the relationship between the teacher and the student.

Teacher: What kind of relationship does it show?

Boy 4: He doesn't act like a teacher though; he acts just like a big, friendly sixth grader!

Girl 3: The more times I talk it doesn't let my student—it's bad.

Boy 5: Why is that bad?

Girl 3 [continues]: It doesn't give the student a chance to learn.

Teacher: Well, maybe we can find out from what John has collected. John has some notes and let's see if he can explain those numbers to us a little better. What numbers did you arrive at yesterday John, and tell us how you arrived at those numbers? Can you do that for us? Is that alright if he shares that with us, Simon?

John: I'll just give the total numbers.

Teacher: Alright.

John: Simon gave out fifty-five and his student gave out fifty-one, and I noticed yesterday he gave out more unit messages in the last half than in the beginning. Henry gave out six in the beginning and seventy-five in the last half and his student gave out twenty-five and thirty-five.

Teacher: So what happened today?

John [continues]: Today it was just the opposite. Henry gave out fifty-two in the first and twenty in the last half; Simon gave out forty in the first half and twenty-three in the last half.

Teacher: What ideas can you gather from these numbers? Do you understand what that means? I heard John say that Henry talked more than one-half of the time and his student talked less than half the time. Maybe we ought to compare that with how much the other teachers talk in relation to their students.

Teacher: What did you notice about the meeting today with so much time spent on the researchers?

[several talk at once]

Boy 7: We talked more about the teachers. I don't care about how much one talks.

Girl 1: That's just your opinion!

Girl 4: We didn't give all of the observers a chance to finish. Not everyone gave their ideas, some talked more than others.

Boy 7: Maybe there's too many observers.

Teacher: What happened in the meeting today? What happened right here in this session while we were discussing; right here in the front of our eyes?

Girl 5: It was kind of different, everybody was interested, and there was lots of moving around—twisting and trying to get their words out.

Boy 8: I observed there was more feedback, it took longer and we didn't have much time for discussion.

Boy 9: At times it was kind of boring.

Girl 6: We jumped around a lot and didn't stay with one topic long enough. . .

Girl 7: Having a lot of feedback gives me more of an understanding of what it is we're doing.

Girl 8: I'd like to have the observations and research kept separate, because when you get interested in the discussion, then you have to quit to hear more observations. We only have a limited amount of time for this meeting.

Recognition of the "limited amount of time" is an indication of the extent to which this twelve-year-old girl had become absorbed in her work and how committed she was to teaching and its improvement. Early in this chapter, I recalled the young principal saying that he was not interested in studying what happened in his school, that he was a *doer* and, by implication, not a thinker. I let teachers off the hook by letting them get away with not being interested in research, just as not having research skills is a cop-out. Now, I've had further thoughts. In my view, every educational administrator and teacher can, and should, orderly study what they are doing and evaluate its effects. That's an integral part of what being professional is all about. If children can become this dedicated to studying *their* impacts, then surely we can expect as much from teachers. And as for that cop-out, there are resources all around if one wants to learn how to evaluate one's performance. More than a decade ago, Beatrice Ward, wrote: "after some twenty-five to thirty years of blindness to the research and development skills and the rich data bases teachers possess, the education research world is recognizing the importance of teachers' inquiry."[27] She cites examples throughout the country of teachers doing research studies in their classrooms—many in collaboration with universities. If one searches diligently enough, there are faculty who would welcome the opportunity to collaborate. They have students who would jump at the chance to have meaningful field work for a change. And every classroom is filled with potential research assistants. There are monies available to aid, just as there is technology that is not being used creatively. Those teachers who are the recipients of the smaller class windfall could have a little more time to take risks and not be caught up with more-of-the-same with fewer children. "I've been teaching for twelve years now," said one New York City teacher who got involved in collaborative research, "and I'm determined not to fall into the rut of an experienced teacher whose most important teaching tool is the file cabinet."[28]

6

Beyond the Procrustean Classroom: A Class of Their Own

> The deepest pleasure an adult can find in life probably comes from what remains in him of his stifled childhood. What an enrichment it would be to the whole of society if childhood, as a specific estate and a separate culture, ceased to be stifled.
>
> Gérard Mendel[1]

> As we look to the future, the only thing we can guarantee our children is that they are going to face massive problems that they will need to solve collaboratively. Solutions might be found in the disciplines if they are viewed not as subjects to be studied but as perspectives on knowing.[2]
>
> Christine Leland and Jerome C. Harste

Having learned some basic methods, in effect, there are no boundaries to what and how children can teach—or what the practice can lead to. Some peer teachers expand their efforts by teaching in pairs, or small groups, while others give demonstration lessons to a whole class. Peer teachers, after they have mastered teaching basic communication skills, often want to enlarge their repertoire; from reading to writing, from math to science; from spelling to social studies, from music and the arts to dance; from conflict resolution, counseling, and enhancing human relations skills, to computers. The classroom inevitably changes. And some move outside its confines. There is no limit when the imagination takes over.

EXTENSIONS

Peer teaching need not be confined to spelling or reading texts. "Content alone," said Laura Fillmore (who runs the Online Bookstore), "fast becomes irrelevant in the absence of context."[3] When children learn a few basic skills and then are given the freedom to use their creativeness, some projects have a way of snowballing, even if they began with limited goals.

Remember that sixth-grade special class in Indiana—the one whose students were seen as average or below grade level in reading and writing? They had been segregated from others their age who showed more academic promise: only five of the twenty-four students said they "sometimes" read books at home. What could the teacher have done to increase their enthusiasm for reading and writing? She, collaborating with a university professor, tried to find out how they could increase their "enthusiasm for reading and writing so that they will engage in literary activities." On a reading attitude survey which the children filled out, they had a question that asked them if they would like to read stories to young children. They answered with such enthusiasm that the teachers decided to pair them with kindergartners—to read to them for 45 minutes weekly. The teachers did not instruct the sixth graders on how to teach reading, but merely told them to have fun reading and writing with the younger children. They held some preparatory meetings about how to maintain a younger child's attention; they came forth with ideas, role-played them, and then discussed what they'd learned. The teachers gave the children the rudiments of plot construction, story elements, and how to map stories. "Working in pairs, sixth graders examined picture books and practiced constructing statements about what happened at the beginning, in the middle, and at the end of the story. . . . Students frequently worked collaboratively to share ideas on mapping a story that had been experienced by the entire group."[4] Next they selected appropriate books, teamed up, and practiced reading to one another with critiques that focused on expression, eye contact, and so on. They role-played suggestions for improvements. Then they began reading to the kindergartners. Following their teaching sessions, they met to critique their work.

But that wasn't all. After several weeks, the tutors wanted to go further. They brainstormed for ideas. At first, they asked their students to tell them about their favorite part of the story, and searched for which characters reminded the listeners of themselves. Then they figured out the plot. The students dictated their replies to the tutors, who, in turn, taught them about story mapping—a devise that *they'd* only recently learned. The students' teacher next suggested dealing with a "theme" she'd noticed common to the young children—that of fear. The tutors again brainstormed the idea, then searched for appropriate books in the library to read to the children. This time they queried the children about the feelings of fear that the characters in the stories had provoked. And then they encouraged their students to come up with stories of their own on the topic. The tutors took dictation from their students, helped them to put it in story mapping format, typed it on computers, and returned with "scripts" for additions, and editing—which *they* were now learning to do as part of their own language arts classes. The peer tutors continued to read stories to the children, enlarging ideas of their own. After more revisions and edits (the sixth graders continued to work in pairs for support and criticism), they added photos and bibliographies of the authors. With the help of mothers, they learned to bind books and so, at the end of the year, presented each of their students with a bound copy and furnished copies to the school library.

The teachers didn't use standardized tests to measure achievement. The sixth graders increased reading on their own by 170 percent. They even petitioned their teacher for more time in class to read. Parents reported that 70 percent of their children were reading on their own. One mother commented that she had "dished out $400 for a complete Nintendo set, and now all he wants to do is read." And by the end of the year, half of the kindergartners brought in their own books written at home. For the first time, the school librarian had waiting lists on books that sixth graders wanted to read and had recommended to their friends. We will only know the mental health value of the project somewhere along the way but perhaps we could calculate it in terms of prevention of aberrant behavior. In terms of enriching the children's lives, its profits are inestimable.

And recall the project in Texas. It showed what can come from a little ingenuity. Those fourth graders initially helped first graders with spelling words from their science lesson each week. They improvised with materials such as "magnetic letters, sandboxes, typewriters, shaving cream, and dry erase boards to practice spelling words correctly."[5] The teachers found, by the way, that there were some first-grade words that the fourth graders couldn't spell. The first graders, however, looked up to their tutors as competent spellers, thereby motivating the latter to learn more.

The project went beyond spelling when the first graders collected spiders to study. The fourth graders helped by locating information on arachnids from the library and then wrote books for their students on the subject. These books, which contained limericks, poems, riddles, and so on, led the tutors to read *Charlotte's Web* first as a class, then to their students, and finally, as a dramatization on video (in the tutors' room). As combined classes, they critiqued the video as to fact and fantasy.

But that exercise only whetted their appetites. Spelling had now become a part of reading. The tutors selected books to read to their students. First, the fourth graders paired off and read to each other for practice and criticized one another for pronunciation and expression. In addition to reading to the first graders, they prepared tapes of books for the children's listening library. The first graders, now aware of evaluation, listened to the book tapes critically; some of the storytellers, the first graders said, sounded like "robots." In turn, the youngsters re-recorded tapes to show their tutors how to be more "lifelike."

The fourth-grade teacher took some of their books and rewrote them in script form and the tutors acted them out. The tutors, likewise (in teams) rewrote sections of the children's stories and put them together, revising and editing a final script. They rehearsed, added costumes, and performed for their students. Next they coached the first graders to act parts of scripts, again costumed. And then the first graders began to show up unannounced in the fourth-grade classroom to show their tutors scripts they'd written on their own.

As with the Indiana students, the fourth graders in Texas moved on to writing books, revising and editing, and working in pairs. They collaborated by taking dictation from their students, who added illustrations. The tutors put the stories on their computers and returned them to the first graders to reedit, correct for spelling, and so on. The end result, again, parallelling the sixth graders in Indiana, was bound books. The tutors interviewed their students and composed biographies, along with photos, which they bound and presented to them for Christmas. Their students reciprocated by compiling song books for their tutors. The younger students were impressed at having books written about them; the older ones felt good to be authors. The parents of both were excited about their children's literary accomplishments. Six and nine year olds worked collaboratively, and as the authors conclude: "a cross-age literacy program makes becoming literate a friendly, natural process as children work together. Reading and writing should not be solitary acts of copying or sounding out, but rather should be fun, group activities."[6]

And then, remember those college athletes in Texas, who teamed up with first and second graders in an elementary school? Those children lived in a neighborhood with a high rate of crime, drug abuse, and poverty. The children were in the "lowest reading groups in their classes and were candidates for retention."[7] The project director selected athletes who'd been admitted to the university, "more on the basis of athletic skill than on academic ability. Many of these students come from impoverished backgrounds, and athletic scholarships have made it possible for them to attend the university."[8] Other university students were tutoring them.

The college students tutored the children for 45–minute sessions two times a week, and, in turn, were taking an evening course at the university in literacy skills and tutoring. They learned story construction (as with the sixth graders in Indiana) and introduced problem-solving procedures to their students in addition to reading. Finally, they wrote, edited, and bound books for their students. The project director operated on the belief that "instruction could be inventive and most effective when tutors were given considerable discretion as to its delivery. . . . While suggested activities and materials were provided, I deliberately did not give the tutors a lock-step method of how to teach the material."[9]

By the end of the semester, 90 percent of the children had moved into a higher reading group in the school. "[M]any of the student athletes told us that it is the first time in their lives they have enjoyed reading and finished reading whole books. . . . Ten tutors [50 percent], because of their positive experiences working with children, have decided to become teachers."[10]

These examples show teachers' using peer teaching creatively and allowing the children and young people to evolve rather than remain static. In the beginning, there was a structure where the trainees acquired a few new skills and a discipline that came from respect. The framework was flexible enough to encourage tutor and student to work collaboratively to accomplish their mission. Then, they moved outward, and the important ingredient of *commitment* emerged. Many, and I would say most, peer teaching projects—at least those reported in the literature—are totally teacher-directed using children to carry out rote methods with limited objectives. They are not very human nor very creative. When content supersedes process, children are deprived of exciting new contextual experiences. Creative peer teaching projects can merge both.

There is no end to the variations and combinations appropriate to peer teaching. Although peer teachers are usually older than their students, the reverse can also be effective as we learned from the Cuban experience. Every community has people and resources untapped for learning. I found a local author of children's books and invited her to come and visit. She became so involved with the children that she came on a weekly basis and had the children write their own stories, which she critiqued. In turn, she had a ready-made laboratory with this young audience who, in turn, critiqued *her* stories-in-progress. A professor at Toledo University (Ohio) got his students together with seniors who'd "lived productive lives" (currently involved in Elderhostel programs) for "intergenerational sessions." "[T]he students were actually engaging the Elderhostelers in conversations about their lives and careers; the seniors, in turn, were seeking information from the young people about their high school classes and activities. . . . In the process, many previous perceptions were leveled."[11]

More and more, we will need children and youth to teach skills to adults such as using computers, learning language (especially where another language is secondary), and participating in the performing arts. Recall Arthur Gillette's remark in the foreword, "With ever-faster evolving technologies and pedagogical methods, there may, in fact, be areas where adults are less effective teachers than youngsters." The new library (located in a shopping mall) in Marin City, California, has put those words into practice. A staff of young WebStars assist library patrons of all ages to learn computer skills (word processing, resumé software, access to the Internet, running search engines, CD ROM discs, and so on). They also create and maintain home pages for local nonprofit groups. The children work in teams. "What one may lack in certain skills or tact," the program director said, "can be filled in by a team member." He was quoted as saying that through teaching, the students will also enhance their communication skills. The WebStars work ten hours a week; those over fourteen years old are paid by the hour and above the minimum wage. Civic officials hope the program and the new library will help to revitalize the community. But for 13-year-old Taniesha Broadfoot, one of the original WebStars, it's more personal: "When you're teaching someone else how to do it, you're teaching yourself."[12]

Similarly, computer experts (many in their teens) could teach older children skills they could then impart to youngsters. Their teachers could supply the important and all-too-neglected analytical and human relations' skills.

A teacher, using the concept imaginatively, can fundamentally change how she teaches and restructure her role in the classroom. One student of mine (a school district art consultant), changed his whole manner of operation. Instead of his former annual sporadic visits to classrooms in the large district, he asked principals to send to his studio students who wanted to learn and practice various art techniques. Then they returned to teach them at their schools. In the intimacy of his workshop, they could see a professional artist at work and learn various procedures by participating with him. They brought in their own works for criticism. In so doing, they gained a further appreciation of art—a total hands-on experience they wouldn't get by visiting an art gallery. The project had an unintended side-effect: mothers who volunteered to transport children to the studio began to participate. Many found a new interest and acted as an inspiring support group for the children while forming a bridge to the school and the teachers.

In the first chapter, I referred to a project sponsored by the University of California Extension on its Riverside campus. This project occurred in the summer of 1965, and, while I realize that it happened more than three decades ago, it showed a different way of learning. I want to use it as an example of extensive peer teaching which crossed several boundaries: race, social class, generations, sex, and formal education.

The project changed the structure of the school itself, and the teachers found a new role for themselves—that of manager, collaborator, trainer, and supporter of growth. Many of the adult peer teachers (or paraprofessionals) came from welfare-dependent households; thus they were finding new opportunities for rewarding jobs.

The 200 volunteer children had limited backgrounds and experiences most of us take for granted—riding on an escalator in a shopping mall, for instance. The children selected one of eight "clusters" they wanted to be with. The four year olds stayed in one group, but the seven other groups had about twenty-five children each, ranging in age from five to twelve. Each group had a teacher and four peer teachers, adults and young adults. Within the group, each assistant teacher had approximately six children who had chosen the teacher they wanted to be with. No one chose one mother, so she found other things to do in her cluster. Each cluster became a learning community (similar in some respects to a one-room school) composed of four smaller working groups; each group was free to work out a program suitable for its members. The project's administrators, however, encouraged maximum use of cross-age teaching both within its cluster and between them. High school and college students, school dropouts, parents, and the children themselves all participated in peer teaching.

Content ranged from the three Rs to sports, arts, experiences from field trips, and so on. Activities in the clusters took place from nine o'clock until noon. Each cluster held a daily discussion group, including the preschoolers (who were separate and held their own discussions). Peer teachers visited the children's homes in the afternoons, attended cluster meetings, or took the children on field trips. And all of the staff met each afternoon at three o'clock for two hours as a group.

We picked the staff one month before the project began; they met one evening each week for orientation and training. Outside trainers gave the total staff an intensive weekend of planning and sensitivity training.

The change and development team, as I said earlier, assisted in training and monitoring the activities of the project. I had trained the two parolees in peer teaching; a month before the regular school adjourned for the summer, they trained twelve fifth graders to tutor first graders. They attempted to measure academic achievement with pre- and posttests, but testing was so threatening to so many of the children there were no reliable results.

The most important consequence was that children *wanted* to come to school—no child dropped out of the project during the summer. Their attendance was voluntary, although I suppose some parents wanted them out of the house for a few hours each day. Some children had to commute over one hour each way by bus. During the school year, children had to be segregated by age and travel on separate buses as the older ones attacked the younger ones. One of the bus drivers had been struck just a few weeks prior to the project. That situation changed rather drastically from the first day; children of all ages rode the buses, and frequently the older ones now continued their teaching with the younger students Some children asked that activities begin an hour earlier so that they would have more time to devote to their work, even though it meant early rising for those who had to take the long bus ride. One child brought a petition to the project director to have the project extended a few more weeks so they could complete their projects.

A team of appraisers from the Bank Street College of Education in New York reported:

> The Aware Team was impressed with the innovative nature of this program, which used a multilevel, intergenerational approach to the problem of communication. . . . There was evidence that learning was taking place among both the children and the total staff—the certified teachers as well as the staff teachers. . . . The affective aspects of the program were perceived. . . to be outstanding, as demonstrated by the openness between staff and teaching assistants and in the planning sessions with children . . . all were significantly involved in an effort to make some basic discoveries about the interactional nature of the learning-teaching process.[13]

We enlarged the project and repeated it the following summer in a primarily Latino community. Some of the peer teachers became trainers. This project also added junior high pupils (as peer teachers, observers, and researchers) and extensive use of video equipment, operated by the children. The visitation team from Bank Street observed:

> Use of junior high students as observers, the use of closed circuit television to record the sessions, cross-age teaching, and the frankly experimental sensitivity training were among the innovative techniques employed and explored in the program, in an attempt to demonstrate the possible roles or functions of both professionals and auxiliaries in a classroom.[14]
>
> Riverside was the only project [of 15 nationwide] in which all ten of the top ranking items were pupil-centered. . . . It is striking that of those ten items, seven were grouped in the sub-cluster as *affective*, and three were subgrouped as *cognitive*. This datum seems even more dramatic when viewed in relation to process. . . . The focus on sensitivity was reinforced in the practicum experience, in the daily review of that experience by auxiliary-teacher teams, and the use of video-taped reproductions of these experiences for purposes of self-evaluation.[15]

HUMAN RELATIONSHIPS THROUGH PEER COUNSELING

It's no side effect that peer teaching helps both tutors and their students with socialization and personality growth. And so, peer teaching need not be confined to traditional subject matter, but may be applied to helping those with behavioral or learning problems, and other areas of counseling.

I first became aware of the power of peer relationships while working on a psychiatric ward at a naval hospital in Japan. We had a small staff who, for the most part, had limited training and experience in treating severely disturbed psychiatric patients. Most of them were the same age and came from similar backgrounds as the patients. As a team, these young hospital corpsmen and nurses (as social therapists) not only were able to communicate with their disturbed peers but also their own attitudes and behavior changed remarkably. One, in particular, wrote of what this experience meant to him.

> A continual effort is maintained to increase communication between staff members and between staff and patients, and in the daily meetings everyone is encouraged to take an active part.

When patients become disturbed, other patients are asked to help them and to contribute suggestions as to how to understand their behavior. The goal is to create an atmosphere where patients will have every opportunity *when they need it most* to communicate with others who are not as disturbed as they are.[16]

It has been noticed that social changes occur in the corpsmen's lives as their working situation changes. . . . Where formerly they frequently talked of "riots," destruction, and other situations charged with anxiety, they now discuss the merits of group therapy and of relating to patients, and compare progress of various patients. Occasionally they review with amusement the anxieties involved in former methods of caring for patients, and point out how much less violence and tension is now present on the entire [psychiatric] service.[17]

This former social therapist bears out the lasting and cumulative effects. When he was discharged from the service, he took a teacher-training course and became an elementary school teacher. It was in his classroom that I observed one of the first peer teaching programs in the mid-1960s. He was applying what he had written about a decade earlier: his children were not only helping one another in their classroom, but also were teaching in the lower grades.

One of the more interesting applications of peer relationships occurred between college freshmen and preadolescent boys. Fifth and sixth graders in California were given the weekly companionship of the freshmen. These were children whose parents were concerned that they were having emotional problems over and beyond the normal pains of growing up. The college men, having successfully gone through many of the same growth experiences, could help the younger boys make the transition more smoothly. A good idea worked! But the college men also experienced the effects. Having mastered the growing pains of adolescence, they were having new ones—those of entering young adulthood. The younger boys, bewildered by all this turmoil, became good listeners—the first essential of skillful therapy. And during the relationship, a number of the college students changed their career plans to those involving people.[18]

I wasn't too surprised to learn these results when I spoke with the project director. I'd recently had experience running a project for youthful, violent offenders in one of California's prisons. Lacking sufficient professional staff, a number of the prisoners, similar to the navy hospital corpsmen, had become adept at helping one another. They evolved a role for themselves over time as "social therapists." They led small groups, counseled and engaged in work and social activities with their fellows. They were especially astute as teachers to the newer prisoners and helped to train new staff.[19]

In the classroom, we've seen extensive use of peers in what might be called preventive measures: conflict resolution, crime and delinquency, substance abuse, sexual orientation and conduct, suicidal preoccupation, and AIDS. Peer participation has taken the form of individual and small group counseling and presentations before large audiences.

SCHOOL AND WORK: A BEGINNING

"Commitment to community," President Clinton avowed, "should be an ethic we should learn as soon as possible so we can carry it throughout our lives." The California Teachers Association's "Blueprint for Educational Excellence" backs the School-to-work/career programs. "[T]hese programs," the plan argues, "must be to prepare students who are employable, socially responsible, and equipped to engage in lifelong learning—for career change and advancement for personal growth."[20]

The crux is *when* and *where* do children learn these traits? Educators have traditionally looked outside to the private sector for learning job-related skills. All the while, we know the business community is highly critical of the graduates from conventional schools. They cite young people's lack of flexibility, communication, and reasoning skills, their inability to work in teams, and their poor attitudes. The industrial world now spends billions annually retraining their work force to enhance productivity.

It's time that educators looked more within the nature of their own classrooms both to better prepare young people for the new world of "work" and to become decent, caring citizens. The current push to boost literacy in the early years offers teachers an incredible opportunity to combine learning to read with peer teaching. At the same time, both tutor and student learn to share responsibility and commitment, to work in groups, and to acquire analytical skills. Herbert Kohl has proposed a different solution to the president's. "The actual skills needed to teach reading," he said in *The Nation*, "are no more complex than the skills needed to repair a car or renovate a house." He suggests:

A new category of school workers whose specialty is literacy can be created. The prerequisites for such people might be as simple as decent reading skills, a sensitive knowledge of the culture and strengths children bring to school, and a level of comfort within poor communities that would allow literacy workers to function in parks, apartments, churches and social service centers, as well as within the relative security of the school building.[21]

While his proposal focuses on adults for this new classification of teachers (beginning with a new Associate of Arts degree from community colleges), the plan could embrace children of all ages. They would not only effectively improve literacy, but the scheme would also give them valuable work experience, perhaps inspiring some to become professional teachers. "What we need is new people in the schools," he concludes, "committed not so much to the world-class standards mouthed by educational professionals as to world-class children."[22] Those new people are already there but they're overlooked as being *mere* children, and they *are* world-class.

Kohl also reminds us that tutoring need not be confined to schools. There are numerous literacy programs being conducted at YWCAs and YMCAs, Big Brothers and Big Sisters, and other nonprofit organizations, which we should expand.

Jeremy Rifkin, in his gripping book, *The End of Work*, shows the increasing role of nonprofit groups both as sources of employment and vehicles for community betterment.[23] Community service for children and youth could be the beginning of an alternative curriculum and method of learning. This type of learning has enormous potential. Whereas vocational training and traditional apprenticeships have had limited appeal to students, teachers, and the work force, human service education could have a much larger constituency and an enormous effect at the same time. The challenge is how to build such experience, which includes peer teaching, into mainstream education. Many of the people working in service organizations have become disillusioned with having students (especially AmeriCorps personnel, young people who are "required" to accumulate hours for graduation, and "offenders" serving in lieu of sentences) join them. As I see it, the main problem which faces the expansion of peer teaching is that both educators and service providers lack the skills to make experience a medium for learning. Experience is not enough. Educators, if they are to meet this challenge, are going have to put in more effort than they have so far. It may take the form of restructuring the school or designing alternatives to learning.

LEARNING COMMUNITIES

I first heard the term "learning community" in the middle 1960s from Maxwell Jones, who was mentioned earlier in a discussion of social learning. He had come to California to give a series of seminars and workshops on prevention and community psychiatry. I invited him to lecture in my classes for teachers and took him to visit projects my students were carrying out in their classrooms. They were experimenting with peer teaching and discussion groups. He was fascinated and quickly entered into the discussions with the teachers and children. When we asked him to elaborate on what he meant by that phrase "learning communities," he only replied that certain basic principles (which he'd developed in therapeutic communities) could apply equally well in the classroom. After all, he said, what he'd done was merely try to establish a climate and develop a set of procedures wherein people could learn from the predicaments in which they found themselves. With the reflections of others in the community, and the freedom to experiment, an immense amount of learning—and application—occurred. He was eager to return to Scotland and try out what he'd seen in the classrooms here.

When I spoke to him years later, he recalled "in the schools in California, I never saw such motivation, such excitement, and such intelligence displayed in children. And the pupils in Scotland picked it up immediately with much the same characteristics." When I asked him how he believed social change could occur on a large scale, he replied:

> In a small, but important way, with peer teaching and discussion groups in the schools. Children can learn at a very young age to take responsibility for helping one another; for understanding, for more intelligent ways to solve daily problems, and for developing a sense of commitment. They can become as competent at solving the problems of daily life as they are in the subject they teach, like maths and language.[24]

It was less than a decade later that he sent me a reprint of an article he'd written with a Denver educator. They'd been experimenting in the schools. The article elucidated his earlier comments about learning communities in schools.[25] He enumerated five components and gave examples of how one could implement them: (1) establishing two-way communication (often "painful" at the moment) between students and teachers and between teachers and administrators; (2) sharing responsibility between administrators, faculty, and students; (3) making schoolwide and classroom decisions by consensus; (4) using everyone's abilities to the maximum;[26] and (5) employing social interaction as a tool for learning.

The phrase "learning community" has become more than another educational soubriquet by Marilyn Watson, who directs the Child Development Project in Oakland, California.[27] Over the past decade, she has focused on constructing "collaborative structures" for classrooms from kindergarten through the secondary grades. She has tested her community-building prototypes in schools through the country and carefully studied its effects. She focuses on four key concepts: (1) fostering caring relationships, beginning with building partnerships between children; (2) teaching humane values through practice by establishing classroom norms; (3) developing intrinsic motivation in contrast to external rewards and punishment; and, (4) teaching within a holistic framework wherein learning is for understanding.[28]

One shouldn't take for granted relationships fundamental to building a learning community as well as for peer teaching; relationships are an integral part of the curriculum. With the concept of interpersonal maturity levels, each child brings into the classroom his own perception of others, her own means of dealing with the web of relationships. The teacher can hone these tendencies, and where necessary, build newer, more utilitarian ones. "In the first class meetings of the year, students discuss 'how we want to be treated by others,' and 'what kind of class we want to be.' From these discussions emerge a few simple principles—'be kind,' 'show respect,' 'do our best,'— that are remarkably similar across diverse schools."[29]

To activate these objectives, students learn to work together as partners (reading to one another is one example), how to interview and practice these skills on each another, and finally, now to collaborate in small groups of two partnerships. Children, by mastering these complexities and absorbing their richness, are then able to function more competently in the classroom community.

Children, in a collaborative classroom community (as with peer teaching), see that learning is for their own sake; its usefulness is both immediate and for the near future.

As teachers, we can try to control children with extrinsic motivators, such as stickers, gold stars, blue ribbons, demerits, names on the board, and Fs. On the other hand, we can prepare children to control themselves by tapping into their intrinsic motivation to learn and to fit in.

Children's intrinsic motivation to figure out and to fit in is not, however, a guarantee that they will want to learn what we are charged with helping them learn, nor that they will want to fit into the classroom community we have designed. . . . Sometimes the community is perhaps too narrowly conceived and needs to be broadened to help children fit in.[30]

"ON THE EDGE OF LEARNING": TRANSMEDIATION

Many, perhaps most, peer teaching programs adhere rather strictly to single subject areas, such as math or language. Most teachers determine both content and method of teaching. Many report significant progress in terms of mastering materials that are testable. But the teacher from New York City (who had become involved in collaborative research) was determined not to fall into the rut of a preselected curriculum. The first-grade teacher, Jeannette (who stopped her peer teaching project), concluded: "We weren't doing anything differently, it wasn't especially enriching, we were all doing the same thing." She failed to realize, however, that peer teaching offers teachers an extraordinary opportunity to experiment. So many children intuitively know how to expand beyond the confines of established ways. There are more holistic patterns of interaction that peer teaching activates. "Collaborative inquiry" is one such way. "We see curriculum as a metaphor for the lives we wish to live and the people we wish to be. To this end, collaborative inquiry is a much-needed curricular frame. . . . Together, disciplines and sign systems provide learners with new perspectives on knowing, foster inquiry, propel learning, and start much-needed conversations."[31]

Christine Leland and Jerome Harste, two university professors, observed a classroom where children moved beyond lineal and linguistic modes of learning; they were able to expand their concepts and imagery.

By concentrating on the new rather than the known, they naturally set themselves up for more learning. . . . They stayed at the edge of their learning because that's where there is always the best chance of learning more. . . . By working on the edge of their competence, where the possibility of failure lurks, mental risk takers are more likely to produce creative results.[32]

"Transmediation" is the term they used when "meanings formed in one communication system are recast in the context and expression planes of a new sign system . . . We see transmediation as a fundamental process in literacy. Movement between and among communication systems provides the opportunity for new perspectives on our knowing and, hence, for the expression of an expanded range of meanings. Transmediation encourages reflection and supports learners in making new connections."[33]

Children are a way to enlarge learning. "[S]tudents are encouraged to choose a topic, explore their personal relationship to the topic, and then use the disciplines as heuristic devices for learning more about the topic . . . questions support children in exploring the potential of a topic, as well as propel them into research as they, more often than not, end up interviewing musicians, visiting art museums, and the like.[34] Or they go on "learning walks."

COLLABORATORIES

How could teachers and tutors use technology to perfect and spread the effects of peer teaching? Could they extend the classroom community into a virtual one—a global community? Two recent technological developments answer those questions. One is in *access*, the other, in *enabling technologies*. The federal government has repeatedly pledged to connect all schools to the Internet. Two software corporations in California have made that pledge a reality; beginning in 1997, all school-age children and youth in that state can have unlimited free e-mail merely by having access to the I-Way.[35]

Now all that waits is the means for children to use that digital reality to form "electronic discussion groups." Here's where William Wulf (professor of computer science at the University of Virginia) comes in. He's proposed a broad-based infrastructure called a "National Collaboratory" (*collaboration* plus *laboratory*). Professor Wulf asks: "[H]ow do people collaborate, and how can we exploit technology to amplify the effectiveness of this collaboration, especially when the collaborators are not collocated?"[36] He envisions an electronic "center without walls," an "invisible university." His view is that technology makes it possible for researchers and scholars to work together as self-selected teams: "Freed from the constraints of distance, opportunity and choice will determine the composition, size and duration of a research team . . . interacting with colleagues, accessing instrumentation, sharing data and computational resources, accessing information in digital libraries."[37]

How can we encourage peer teachers to mount those heights? The sixth graders, who were searching for means to objectify their observations and check assumptions, were already well on the road to using scientific methodology. There is in place a prototype to further such beginnings. The "Collaborative Notebook"[38] project at Northwestern University is a means to bring high school science students together using computer-visualization tools instead of textbooks and lectures. Teachers could easily adapt this arrangement for peer teachers of any age. They already know the value of teamwork and have become skillful in its usage. If you will recall that as Bill (the twelve-year-old, cross-age teacher in my classroom) became proficient, he extended his knowledge to teaching and consulting with others. He then searched nearby schools for new ideas to bring back to our classroom. Creative use of technology means that there is a method and an infrastructure already available to expand such endeavors. Peer tutors and their teachers could exchange ideas, coordinate their work, and engage in mutual training and research. They could devise chat-rooms, message boards, and MUDs[39] (virtual role-playing) to create on-line peer teaching communities: working, action communities with the mission of building, testing, and modifying prototypes. Teachers and peer teachers could build and use their knowledge to the extent that such social construction would allow. They could adapt other available techniques, such as interactive-video conferencing, and distance learning to extend peer teaching. Children and their teachers could connect via phone lines with television to engage in live exchanges with one another. They could transmit teaching sessions, critiques, and discussion groups to other like-minded children and interact with them live in a virtual community. These facilities are already available at universities in many parts of the country.[40] Phoenix College in Arizona actually has an interactive laboratory (a MUD) for on-line global learning.[41]

Earlier in this chapter, I spoke of learning communities. We hear "community" used in a variety of contexts. When Marshall McLuhan introduced the phrase, "global community" (in the 1960s), he was referring both to the "electronic information environment," and "the new age of tribal involvement."[42] That union has born the extensive use of e-mail. People communicate with one another anonymously in the most intimate of terms from around the globe: "neighbors in cyberspace." "In spite of its relatively long history, new users of e-mail are often surprised—by things people say in e-mail they would never say in person."[43] Humans have a basic urge to communicate with one another. One could archetypically trace the longing to hear and be heard to Hermes,[44] the Greek messenger god. The archetype takes many forms revealing its presence in the matchmaker, the pen pal, the tattletale, and the informant.[45] It is natural, therefore, that children take to e-mail. It allows them to make contact with others away from their immediate environment. Some will caution that children could be exploited— the negative side of the archetype—and that situation, indeed, has happened. Teachers, freed from some instruction, can minimize the possible misuse of this freedom to communicate, and can collaborate with their students so that communication stays open and is not driven underground. Daily classroom community meetings are one way. Jointly, older children working with younger ones in cross-age relationships can also aid in keeping communication unclosed, yet vital.

Children, in like manner, could build their own working or action communities—"dynamic neighborhoods."[46] They could enlarge their experiences, exchange ideas, and propose and carry out collaborative projects. Although school-age children in California now have free access to e-mail, many in other states and countries have access through their schools, public libraries, and various institutions.

Lynn Conway, professor of electrical engineering and computer science at the University of Michigan, developed a "community of designers" that might give some clues about how to develope a "community of peer teachers."[47] Basically it involved the use of e-mail as a device for creating and maintaining such an endeavor. Professor Conway needed a way to test new design methods. She drafted a textbook on her ideas, distributed it to others for their views, marketed it, kept track of the schools who used it, and thus built a constituency. Using e-mail, she was able to keep in contact with people in these schools, put them in touch with one another so they could share designs and materials, and test out prototypes. She could "fan out" ideas to any number of those in her working community and they could do the same.

> E-mail knitted the community of designers into an organic whole in which the processes of knowledge creation, propagation, and testing ran much faster than they usually do. . . . As participants got to know each other, they became a community. [The project] is about the social construction and use of knowledge. . . people with a mission could coordinate their work and collaborate in creating wider knowledge. . . . "[T]he draft textbook, became the languages that defined and knitted together a new community."[48]

MEDIA LITERACY

Initially, I remarked on the expansion of literacy to include emotional and ethical concepts. Xerox's principal scientist, Mark Stefik reminds us that literacy "is largely a consequence of the nineteenth-century creation of public schools."[49] Since that time, we have expanded our notions of literacy. Today, we are embracing "digital literacy"—needed "to watch a movie, listen to music, or use a computer program—different from the literacy required to read a book."[50] The former CEO of Silicon Graphics, one of the major computer software firms, has been so daring as to put forward an eight-fold curriculum for children to qualify for an "Information Superhighway Driver's License." Attainment of these skills, he says, "would extend beyond individual classrooms, with students having a positive influence on other generations: . . . true universal access is dependent on the next generation of Americans: today's children." It's worth replicating his curriculum because each of the components carries with it important implications for peer teaching. I cite this "curriculum" as it enhances skills of communication, interpersonal relationships, and, as I have suggested, integrates technology with intellectual endeavors—all components of a successful peer teaching program. CEO McCracken proposes that all ten year olds should be able to:

- Gain access to at least one on-line service.
- Establish a personal Internet address as an introduction to electronic mail.
- Collaborate with students in other countries in order to learn about their cultures.
- Use the on-line catalog of a local library as well as the Library of Congress to research a homework project.
- Search computer networks using file transfer methods and copy free software to their computer. As part of this exercise, students could be exposed to the ethical and legal considerations involved in concepts such as intellectual property rights as well as computer security and privacy issues.
- Participate in a news group discussion to communicate with others in various locations.
- Access a local bulletin board system to gather and download multimedia information on topics being studied in school.
- Monitor government services or legislative actions at the state, local or federal level, and send a letter to an elected representative.[51]

CHILDREN AND YOUTH FOR THE YEAR 2000

In Athens, education was not a segregated activity, conducted for certain hours, in certain places, at a certain time of life. It was the aim of the society. The city educated the man. The Athenian was educated by the culture, by *paideia*.

Robert Hutchins

What could we expect if young people were no longer restricted from having significant and purposeful experiences? What would happen, instead, if at an early age, they were offered new opportunities to participate in society by helping others?

- For one thing, our image of children and youth would change from that of being careless, troublesome, and invisible, to one of responsible, contributing members of society.

- Children might begin to look for new modes of encounter and means to prepare themselves for more creative occupations as our world of material abundance rapidly changes.

- In time, they might no longer be content with the status quo. They would begin to question and experiment with the way traditional institutions work—schools, youth-serving agencies, religion, government, politics, and families.

- That shift would enable children and young people to become intellectually and emotionally empowered—thus knowledgeable—to make contributions for change and, in turn, to take more leadership and initiative in making these changes.

- As our institutions changed, youth would have more real power over their lives and destinies, greater independence, their own money and purchasing power, as well as power to fashion goods, services, leisure, and entertainment.

- As for prevention, as Maxwell Jones said, psychiatry and social work would simply disappear!

It seems an incongruity that we should speak of children and youth as "generation X" as if it were an undiscovered chromosome or some other nondescript chemical body. And yet, we have lost touch with youth and their potentials to such an extent that the analogy may prove apt. Youth mirror the circumstances of our times: from the activism that characterized the 1960s, to the silence that prevailed during the 1980s. Our social context has shifted so radically in the past decade that perhaps being labeled as "X" (the unknown) will allow them to define their own place. As we approach the next millennium, there is still time to change fundamentally the way we live in the world community—to the benefit of us all. As Professor Bruner wrote: "education is in constant process of invention. . . . [E]ach generation must define afresh the nature, direction, and aims of education to assure such freedom and rationality as can be attained for a future generation."[52]

Farid Senzal from Afghanistan attended the United Nations' 50th anniversary celebration in San Francisco in 1995. This twenty-one year old said, "We inherit a world of pain and suffering, oppression and abuse.

These are pressing issues which we must address. National borders are increasingly unimportant. We must all work together, across political lines, across social and economic lines, and indeed across religious lines. [Youth] have the vision, the power and the faith to make our dream a reality. I am excited for the future."[53]

Quite frankly, I am too!

Notes

INTRODUCTION

1. Herbert Kohl, "Saving Public Education," *The Nation*, February 17, 1997, 23. See also Kohl's recent book, *I Won't Learn from You* (New York: New Press, 1994).

2. Vernon L. Allen and Robert S. Feldman, "Studies on the Role of Tutor," in *Children as Teachers: Theory and Research on Tutoring*, ed. Vernon L. Allen (New York: Academic Press, 1976), 114.

3. Jerome Bruner, *Toward a Theory of Instruction* (Cambridge, Mass.: Harvard University Press, 1966), 128.

4. Ibid., 38.

CHAPTER 1

1. William Bentley Fowle, quoted in Alan Gartner, Mary Kohler, and Frank Riessman, *Children Teach Children: Learning by Teaching* (New York: Harper and Row, 1971), 16.

2. Peggy Lippitt, "Children Can Teach Other Children," *The Instructor* (May 1969): 41; Peggy Lippitt and John E. Lohman, "A Neglected Resource—Cross-Age Relationships," *Children* (May–June 1965): 113–17.

3. Robert Cloward, "Teenagers as Tutors of Academically Low-Achieving Children: Impact on Tutors and Tutees," in *Children as Teachers: Theory and Research on Tutoring*, ed. Vernon L. Allen (New York: Academic Press, 1976), 219–30.

4. Ralph Melaragno, "The Tutorial Community," in *Children as Teachers: Theory and Research on Tutoring*, ed. Vernon L. Allen (New York: Academic Press, 1976), 189–97.

5. Arthur Gillette, *One Million Volunteers: The Story of Volunteer Youth Service* (Harmondsworth, Middlesex: Penguin, 1968), 54.

6. Ibid., 55.

7. Arthur Gillette, *Youth and Literacy: You've Got a Ticket to Ride* (Paris: Unesco, 1973). See also, Jonathan Kozol, *Children of the Revolution* (New York: Delacorte, 1980).

8. "Strengthening of the Role of Teachers in a Changing World: Celebration of the One-hundredth Anniversary of the Birth of Célestin Freinet (1896–1996)," Document: ED/BIE/CONFINTED .45/Inf.11 (Geneva: International Bureau of Education, August 1996).

9. Dennie Briggs, *New Careers for Non-Professionals in Education, Final Report* (Riverside: University of California Extension, 1965), 270 pages.

10. Vernon L. Allen, ed., *Children as Teachers: Theory and Research on Tutoring* (New York: Academic Press, 1976), 17–18.

CHAPTER 2

1. John O'Neil, "On Emotional Intelligence: A Conversation with Daniel Goleman," *Educational Leadership* 54 (September 1996): 6.

2. Daniel Goleman, *Emotional Intelligence: Why It Can Matter More than IQ* (New York: Bantam Books, 1995), 262.

3. Daniel Goleman estimates that "IQ contributes, at best, about 20 percent to the factors that determine life success. That leaves 80 percent to everything else." Quoted in O'Neil, "On Emotional Intelligence," 6.

4. Howard Gardner, *Frames of Mind: The Theory of Multiple Intelligences* (New York: Basic Books, 1983), 254.

5. Ibid., 274–75.

6. Honorable mention article Charles Lee wrote that appeared in the *San Francisco Chronicle*, May 5, 1997.

7. Gardner, *Frames of Mind*, 357.

8. Ibid.

9. Ibid., 274.

10. Maxwell Jones, *Beyond the Therapeutic Community: Social Learning and Social Psychiatry* (New Haven: Yale University Press, 1968), 70, 73, 94.

11. Ibid., 101.

12. Dennie Briggs, "Social Learning—A Holistic Approach: A Conversation With Maxwell Jones," *Journal of Holistic Nursing* 6 (1988): 33.

13. For this presentation, I have omitted the two beginning levels found mainly in infants; as children and adults these integration levels are found in those who are autistic or severely mentally impaired. Likewise those in the two highest levels are not too commonly found in the classroom. There are exceptions to these categories, of course, and there are those who are on the fringes. But the majority of children and young adults resemble the characteristics of those in the middle three integration levels. As growth occurs, there can be movement to higher levels of integration.

14. Clyde Sullivan, Marguerite Grant, and J. Douglas Grant, "The Development of Interpersonal Maturity: Applications to Delinquency," *Psychiatry* 20 (1957): 373.

15. Ibid., 375.

16. Ibid., 374.

17. Ibid., 379.

18. Ibid., 381.

19. Ibid., 382.

20. Ibid., 383–84. A more extensive discussion of other typologies is contained in an article by Jane Loevinger, "Personality: Stages, Traits, and the Self," *Annual Review of Psychology* 34 (1983):195–222. The personality integration concept is not unlike Eric Erikson's evolutionary stages of growth that he proposes must be solved in the course of development of the life cycle.

21. Robert Sternberg, "Thinking Styles: Keys to Understanding Student Performance," *Phi Delta Kappan* (January 1990): 366.

22. Ibid., 369, emphasis in original.

23. Ibid., 371. An excellent recap on learning styles is to be found in *Educational Leadership* (October 1990), which devoted an entire issue to that subject with interviews of some of its leading exponents.

24. Charles Schroeder, "New Students—New Learning Styles," *Change* (September/October 1993): 23–24.

25. Ibid., 24.

26. Ibid.

27. "Jung used 'extravert' to describe an attitude characterized by a flow of psychic energy toward the outer world or toward the object, leading to an interest in events, people, things and a dependency on them. For the introvert, the flow of psychic energy is inward, the concentration is on subjective factors and inner responses." Jean Shinoda Bolen, *Gods in Everyman: A New Psychology of Men's Lives and Loves* (San Francisco: Harper & Row, 1989), 10.

28. Schroeder, "New Students—New Learning Styles," 26.

29. Theodore Sarbin, "Cross-Age Tutoring and Social Identity," *Children as Teachers: Theory and Research on Tutoring*, ed. Vernon L. Allen (New York: Academic Press, 1976), 35.

30. Ann F. Mann, "College Peer Tutoring Journals: Maps of Development," *Journal of College Student Development* 35 (1994): 168.

31. Ibid.

32. Ibid., 167–68.

CHAPTER 3

1. Peggy Lippitt, "Children Can Teach Other Children," *Instructor* 9 (May 1969): 41.

2. Peggy Lippitt, *Students Teach Students*. (Bloomington, Ind.: Phi Delta Kappa Educational Foundation, 1975), 31.

3. Alan Gartner, Mary Kohler, and Frank Riessman, *Children Teach Children: Learning By Teaching* (New York: Harper and Row, 1971), 120.

4. Ibid., 109, emphasis in original.

5. If video equipment is available, it is useful to tape the training sessions, using instant replay to capture behavior as it occurs for discussion. Teachers and trainees can also review segments independently and in future training meetings. Learning to operate the camera and record interactions helps trainees to be more observant and objective in their interpretations.

6. Ibid., 110–11.

7. Eric Trist, "Transition to a Neo-Industrial Society," paper presented at the World Federation for Mental Health meetings, Edinburgh, September 1969.

8. Gartner, Kohler, and Riessman, *Children Teach Children*, 111, emphasis in original.

CHAPTER 4

1. Ann F. Mann, "College Peer Tutoring Journals: Maps of Discovery," *Journal of College Student Development* (May 1994): 168.

2. Ibid., 166.

3. Vernon L. Allen and Robert Feldman, "Studies on the Role of Tutor," *Children as Teachers: Theory and Research in Tutoring*, ed. Vernon L. Allen (New York: Academic Press, 1976), 119.

4. R. N. Bush, et al., *Microteaching: A Description* (Stanford, Calif.: The University Press, 1968).

5. Training materials for teachers include, *That's My Buddy! Friendship and Learning Across the Grades; That's My Buddy! Collegial Study Guide*, and an accompanying videotape. The program was developed, fieldtested, and modified over a twelve-year period in ten schools in different parts of the country. Developmental Studies Center, 2000 Embarcadero, Suite 305, Oakland, CA 94606–5300. Telephone: (800) 666–7270; www.devstu.org.

6. *That's My Buddy! Collegial Study Guide*, 38–39; see also, Catherine Lewis, Eric Schaps, and Marilyn Watson, "The Caring Classroom's Academic Edge," *Educational Leadership* (September 1966): 16–21. To expand peer teaching into other areas and to acquire further skills, such as interviewing, conceptualizing, classifying, "mind mapping," physical activities,and graphic arts, see Developmental Studies Center, *Blueprints for a Collaborative Classroom: 250 Activity Suggestions*.

7. Charles R. Greenwood and Joseph Delquadri, "ClassWide Peer Tutoring and the Prevention of School Failure," *Preventing School Failure* 39 (1995): 22.

8. Ibid., 24.

9. Katherine Samway, Gail Whang, and Mary Pippitt, *Buddy Reading: Cross-age Tutoring in a Multicultural School* (Portsmouth, N.H.: Heinemann, 1995).

10. Douglas Rushkoff, *Playing With the Future: How Kids' Culture Can Teach Us to Thrive in an Age of Chaos* (New York: HarperCollins, 1996), 213.

11. Dennie Briggs, "Older Children Teaching Youngers," *Journal of the California Teachers' Association* (January 1967): 26.

CHAPTER 5

1. Brenda S. Engel, "Portfolio Assessment and the New Paradigm: New Instruments and New Places," *The Educational Forum* 50 (1994): 24.

2. Gregory Bateson, "Appendix C: Consultants' Evaluation of the Program," in Harry Wilmer, *Social Psychiatry in Action: A Therapeutic Community* (Springfield, Ill.: Charles C. Thomas, 1958), 349.

3. Engel, "Portfolio Assessment," 24.

4. Ibid.

5. The principal, impressed with the performance—and enthusiasm—of the sixth graders, proposed that they use their newly found expertise to help children in the lower grades who were having difficulties with math. Displaced by their success, the junior high math teachers had to find new jobs. And so they moved on to help their former students become teachers—to teach them some of the tricks of the trade they'd learned by experience and from observing their own teachers.

6. H. M. Levin, G. V. Glass, and G. R. Meister, *The Cost-effectiveness of Four Educational Interventions* (Stanford, Calif.: The University Institute for Research on Educational Finance and Governance, 1984), ERIC Document ED 246 533.

7. Engel, "Portfolio Assessment," 24.

8. Ibid., 27.

9. Carol DeRita and Susan Weaver, "Cross-Age Literacy Program," *Reading Improvement* (1991): 245.

10. Adapted from: Stephenia Arness, ed., *What You Need Is Program Development: A Student Guide to Successful Programs* (San Rafael, Calif.: Social Action Research Center, 1978), developed as part of "Training for Youth Participation in Program Development Project" (Grant #78–JN-AX-0013), U.S. Department of Justice, Office of Juvenile Justice and Delinquency Prevention.

11. J. Douglas Grant, "The Psychologist as an Agent for Scientific Approaches to Social Change," in *Progress in Clinical Psychology*, ed. L. Abt and T. Riess (New York: Grune and Stratton, 1966), 42.

12. Port (to carry), folio (papers; book of such papers). Professors Terri Wenzlaff and Katharine Cummings define a portfolio as: "a collection that relates to one or more dimensions of a person's professional life: methods used, artifacts of the work itself, feelings about the work, and indicators of professional growth. . . each piece of evidence must be collected or created and organized in a compelling manner to demonstrate proficiency in or progress toward a purpose." Terri Wen -

zlaff and Katharine Cummings, "The Portfolio as Metaphor for Teacher Reflection," *Contemporary Education* (Winter 1996): 109.

There are numerous guides for constructing portfolios available from educational publishers. If these handbooks are not followed devoutly, children can be quite imaginative in how they "package" their portfolios which amounts to "selling" themselves as tutors.

13. Wenzlaff and Cummings, "The Portfolio as Metaphor for Teacher Reflection," 111.

14. Ibid.

15. Ibid., 109.

16. Engel, "Portfolio Assessment," 25.

17. Deborah Meier, *The Power of Their Ideas: Lessons for America from a Small School in Harlem* (Boston: Beacon, 1995), 109.

18. Ibid., 49.

19. Ibid., 50.

20. ibid., 65.

21. Toni Sills-Briegel, Candace Fisk, and Vicki Dunlop, "Graduation by Exhibition," *Educational Leadership* 55 (December/January 1996–1997): 70.

22. Ibid., 71.

23. Jeannette Hartman, Emily DeCicco, and Gayle Griffin, "Urban Students Thrive as Independent Researchers," *Educational Leadership* (November 1994): 46.

24. Ibid.

25. Ibid., 47.

26. The system was a modification of "interaction process analysis," which was developed by Professor Robert Bales at Harvard. A message unit was a judgment of a separate idea which was spoken, whether one word or many. It could come in the form of a statement, a fragment of one, or a question. Message units were simply tallied for the teacher and the student separately and a percentage was calculated.

To study attention span, the children merely made judgments on when it appeared that the student (or teacher) showed signs of distraction. At this particular time, the teaching sessions consisted of 20 to 30 minutes with a brief break midway.

27. Beatrice Ward, "Do You Think of Yourself as a Teacher-Researcher? You Should!" *American Educator* (Fall 1984): 38.

28. Ibid., 39.

CHAPTER 6

1. See Gérard Mendel's Introduction to *Rights and Responsibilities of Youth* (Paris: Unesco Educational Studies and Documents, Number 6, 1972), 8.

2. Christine Leland and Jerome C. Harste, "Multiple Ways of Knowing: Curriculum in a New Key," *Language Arts* (September 1994): 344.

3. Laura Fillmore, "Excerpt from 'Slaves of a New Machine: Exploring the For-Free/For-Pay Condrum,' " in Mark Stefik, *Internet Dreams: Archetypes, Myths, and Metaphors* (Cambridge: The MIT Press, 1996), 215.

4. Christine Leland and Ruth Fitzpatrick, "Cross-Age Interaction Builds Enthusiasm for Reading and Writing," *The Reading Teacher* (December 1993/January 1994): 296.

5. Carol DeRita and Susan Weaver, "Cross-Age Literacy Program" *Reading Improvement* 28 (1991): 245.

6. Ibid., 248.

7. Connie Juel, "Cross-Age Tutoring Between Student Athletes and At-Risk Children," *The Reading Teacher* (November 1991): 183.

8. Ibid., 178.

9. Ibid., 181.

10. Ibid., 184.

11. Mark Kinney, "A Breath of Second Spring in the Social Studies Classroom," *The Social Studies* (January/February 1993): 43.

12. Jim Doyle, "Wanted: High-Tech Teens. Marin City Recruits Kids to Teach Web," *San Francisco Chronicle*, February 12, 1997.

13. Gordon Klopf and Garda Bowman, *Teacher Education in a Social Context* (New York: Bank Street College of Education, 1966), 64–65.

14. Garda Bowman and Gordon Klopf, *New Careers and Roles in the American School: Report of Phase One; A Study of Auxiliary Personnel in Education* (New York: Bank Street College of Education, 1967), 130–31.

15. Ibid., 130.

16. Rodney Odgers, "Experiences with Advances in Psychiatric Patient Care," *U.S. Naval Medical Technician's Bulletin* (November-December 1956): 249.

17. Ibid., 250.

18. Gerald Goodman, "Companionship as Therapy: The Use of Nonprofessional Talent," in *New Directions in Client Centered Therapy*, ed. Joseph Hunt and T. M. Tomlinson (Boston: Houghton Mifflin, 1970), 349–71.

19. Stuart Whiteley, Dennie Briggs, and Merfyn Turner, *Dealing with Deviants: The Treatment of Antisocial Behavior* (New York: Schocken, 1973). See chapters 4, 5, and 6.

20. California Teachers Association, "Blueprint for Educational Excellence," *California Educator* (April 1997): 14.

21. Herbert Kohl, "Saving Public Education," *The Nation*, February 17, 1997, 23.

22. Ibid.

23. Jeremy Rifkin says, "The Third Sector [nonprofits] is the bonding force, the social glue that unites the diverse interest of the American people into a cohesive social identity. . . . The assets of the Third Sector now equal nearly half

the assets of the federal government. A study conducted in the 1980s estimated that the expenditure of America's nonprofit voluntary organizations exceeded the gross national product of all but seven nations. . . . [I]t has been growing twice as fast as both the government and market sectors." Jeremy Rifkin, "Rethinking the Purpose of Education: Preparing Students for 'The End of Work,' " *Educational Leadership* (February 1997): 32. See his *The End of Work: The Dawn of the Post-Market Era* (New York: Putnam, 1995).

24. Dennie Briggs, *The Therapeutic Community: Dialogues with Maxwell Jones, MD* (San Francisco: University of California Library Special Collections, 1991), 149.

25. Maxwell Jones and Gene Stanford, "Transforming Schools into Learning Communities," *Phi Delta Kappan* (November 1973): 201–23.

26. "[R]ole reversal in the form of 'cross-age teaching' can be initiated. . . . Discussion of the problems encountered in helping these younger pupils offers rich opportunities for learning; students develop closer rapport with their own teacher. They begin to empathize with him and better understand his difficulties in keeping discipline and managing the classroom." Ibid., 203.

27. The Developmental Studies Center offers study packages, including books and videotapes for teachers, of carefully designed methods to build and maintain collaborative classroom communities. Development Studies Center, 2000 Embar - cadero, Suite 305, Oakland, CA 94606–5300.

28. Joan Dalton and Marilyn Watson, *Among Friends: Classrooms Where Caring and Learning Prevail* (Oakland, Calif.: Developmental Studies Center, 1997), 9–95.

29. Catherine Lewis, Eric Schaps, and Marilyn S. Watson, "The Caring Class - room's Academic Edge," *Educational Leadership* (September 1996): 18.

30. Dalton and Watson, *Among Friends*, 65.

31. Christine Leland and Jerome Harste, "Multiple Ways of Knowing: Cur - riculum in a New Key," *Language Arts* (September 1994): 344.

32. McAleer, quoted in ibid., 343.

33. Ibid., 340.

34. Ibid., 341.

35. Wendy Tanaka, "E-mail Free For State's Students," *San Francisco Chron - icle*, March 13, 1997.

36. William Wulf, "The National Collaboratory—A White Paper," in Mark Stefik, *Internet Dream: Archetypes, Myths, and Metaphors* (Cambridge: The MIT Press, 1996), 347.

37. Ibid., 346.

38. Developed at the School of Education and Social Policy and Institute for the Learning Sciences at Northwestern University. Their projects are designed around a format that: "*gives students tools they can use to discuss the research they perform with one another and with distant researchers and educators. . . . Students can keep private journals and group notebooks and conduct public discussions on the net-*

work." (Stefik, *Internet Dreams*, 351, emphasis in original.) Their web site is: http://www.covis.nwu.edu/papers/emedia94.html.

39. A MUD is a "multiuser dungeon, or domain, or dimension. . . . a virtual space, accessible via the Internet, where players participate in a new kind of social virtual reality. MUDs are organized around the metaphor of physical space and allow participants to create new, often anonymous identities." Constance Hale, *Wired Style: Principles of English Usage in the Digital Age* (San Francisco: Hardwired Books, 1996), 73–74. As some have suggested, they form a new kind of commu - nity.

40. The Interactive University Project at the University of California in Berkeley has linked children in kindergarten through high school with university students and professors. The children from five to eighteen will also have use of the university library, join chat groups with visiting scholars, have student men - tors, and on-line connections worldwide with projects, including NASA. They will be connected with other students through videoconferencing. Julian Guthrie, "School Kids Gain UC-Berkeley Linkup," *San Francisco Examiner*, October 16, 1996. Nanette Asimov, "Mentoring via Internet For Kids in S.F., Oakland," *San Francisco Chronicle*, October 15, 1996.

41. Stefik, *Internet Dreams*, 351.

42. Marshall McLuhan and Quentin Fiore, *War and Peace in the Global Village* (New York: Bantam Books, 1968), 5. Reissued by Hardwired Books, 520 Third Street, San Francisco, 1996.

43. Stefik, *Internet Dreams*, 114.

44. One of the first e-mail systems on the military network that preceded the Internet (between 1975 and 1977) was named Hermes (Stefik, *Internet Dreams*, 113). See Part 2 ("The Electronic Mail Metaphor: I-Way As a Communications Medium") in Stefik for an interesting discussion of the effects of e-mail.

45. Ibid., 113.

46. Douglas Rushkoff, *Playing with the Future: How Kids' Culture Can Teach Us to Thrive in an Age of Chaos* (New York: HarperCollins, 1996), 26.

47. Lynn Conway, "Excerpt from 'The MPC Adventures: Experiences with the Generation of VLSI Design and Implementation Methodologies,' " in Mark Stefik, *Internet Dreams: Archtypes, Myths, and Metaphors* (Cambridge: The MIT Press, 1996), 143–59.

48. Stefik, *Internet Dreams*,158–59, emphasis in original.

49. Ibid., 7.

50. Ibid., 9.

51. Edward McCracken, "Giving Kids Computer Access," *San Francisco Chronicle*, October 17, 1994.

52. Jerome Bruner, *Toward a Theory of Instruction* (Cambridge, Mass.: Harvard University Press, 1966), 127.

53. Farid Senzal, "Youth, People and Tragedies of War," *San Francisco Chronicle*, June 30, 1995.

Suggested Readings

BOOKS

Allen, Vernon L., ed. *Children as Teachers: Theory and Research on Tutoring*. New York: Academic Press, 1976.

Gartner, Alan, Mary Kohler, and Frank Riessman. *Children Teach Children: Learning by Teaching*. New York: Harper and Row, 1971.

Goleman, Daniel. *Emotional Intelligence: Why It Can Matter More Than IQ*. New York: Bantam Books, 1995.

Rushkoff, Douglas. *Playing with the Future: How Kids' Culture Can Teach Us to Thrive in an Age of Chaos*. New York: HarperCollins, 1996.

Samway, Katherine, Gail Whang, and Mary Pippitt. *Buddy Reading: Cross-age Tutoring in a Multicultural School*. Portsmouth, N.H.: Heinemann, 1995.

Stefik, Mark. *Internet Dreams: Archetypes, Myths, and Metaphors*. Cambridge, Mass.: The MIT Press, 1996.

Wilkes, Roberta. *Peer and Cross-Age Tutoring and Related Topics: an Annotated Bibliography*. (Theoretical Paper No. 53). Madison WI: Wisconsin Research and Development Center for Cognitive Learning, The University of Wisconsin, 1975.

ARTICLES

Briggs, Dennie. "A Method of Peer Teaching for School Children." *Prospects* 6 (Unesco) (1976): 458–69.

———. "Let the Children Teach." *San Francisco Examiner*, September 20, 1966.

———. "Trends in Learning in the United States: A Passing Glance." *Prospects* 25 (Unesco) (September 1995): 373–91

_____ . "Turning Conflicts into Learning Experiences." *Educational Leadership* 54 (September 1996): 60–63.

_____ . "Every Child a Teacher." *Christian Science Monitor*, September 17, 1996.

_____ . "A Bully Transformed by Trust: A 12-Year Old Discipline Problem Becomes a 'Teacher's Aide' to Second Graders." *Los Angeles Times*, December 28, 1996.

De Rita, Carol, and Susan Weaver. "Cross-Age Literacy Program." *Reading Improvement* 28 (1991): 244–48.

Engel, Brenda S. "Portfolio Assessment and the New Paradigm: New Instruments and New Places." *The Educational Forum* 59 (1994): 22–27.

Hartman, Jeanette, Emily K. Decicco, and Gayle Griffin. "Urban Students Thrive as Independent Researchers." *Educational Leadership* 52 (November 1994): 46–47.

Juel, Connie. "Cross-Age Tutoring between Student Athletes and At-Risk Children." *The Reading Teacher* 45 (November 1991): 178–87.

Leland, Christine, and Ruth Fitzpatrick. "Cross-Age Interaction Builds Enthusiasm for Reading and Writing." *The Reading Teacher* 47 (December 1993/January 1994): 292–301.

Leland, Christine, and Jerome C. Harste. "Multiple Ways of Knowing: Curriculum in a New Key." *Language Arts* 71 (1994): 337–45.

Lewis, Catherine, Eric Schaps, and Marilyn Watson. "The Caring Classroom's Academic Edge." *Educational Leadership* 54 (September 1996): 16–21.

Mann, Ann F. "College Peer Tutoring Journals: Maps of Development." *Journal of College Student Development* 35 (May 1994): 164–69.

Riessman, Frank. "Students Teaching Students." *In These Times* (June 27, 1994).

Riessman, Frank, and Audrey J. Gartner. "Tutoring Helps Those Who Give, Those Who Receive." *Educational Leadership* 52 (September 1994): 58–60.

Schroeder, Charles. "New Students—New Learning Styles." *Change* 25 (September/October 1993): 21–26.

Ward, Beatrice A. "Do You Think of Yourself as a Teacher-Researcher? You Should!" *American Educator* (Fall 1984): 38–42.

Wenzlaff, Terri, and Katharine Cummings. "The Portfolio as Metaphor for Teacher Reflection." *Contemporary Education* 67 (Winter 1996): 109–12.

Index

About the Author

DENNIE BRIGGS has taught at San Francisco State University, Governors State University in Illinois, the North London Polytechnic, and University of California Extension. He is the author of more than 100 articles in professional journals and the media.

ISBN 0-89789-550-9

EAN

9 780897 895507

HARDCOVER BAR CODE